Studying the Built Environment

Palgrave Study Guides

Authoring a PhD
Career Skills
e-Learning Skills
Effective Communication for Arts and
    Humanities Students
Effective Communication for Science and
    Technology
The Foundations of Research
The Good Supervisor
How to Manage your Arts, Humanities
    and Social Science Degree
How to Manage your Distance and Open
    Learning Course
How to Manage your Postgraduate
    Course
How to Manage your Science and
    Technology Degree
How to Study Foreign Languages
How to Write Better Essays
Making Sense of Statistics
The Mature Student's Guide to Writing
The Postgraduate Research Handbook

Presentation Skills for Students
The Principles of Writing in Psychology
Professional Writing
Research Using IT
Skills for Success
The Student's Guide to Writing
The Study Skills Handbook (2nd edn)
Study Skills for Speakers of English as a
    Second Language
Studying the Built Environment
Studying Economics
Studying History (2nd edn)
Studying Mathematics and its
    Applications
Studying Modern Drama (2nd edn)
Studying Physics
Studying Psychology
Teaching Study Skills and Supporting
    Learning
Work Placements – A Survival Guide for
    Students
Writing for Engineers

Palgrave Study Guides: Literature

General Editors: John Peck and Martin Coyle

How to Begin Studying English Literature
    (3rd edn)
How to Study a Jane Austen Novel (2nd
    edn)
How to Study a Charles Dickens Novel
How to Study Chaucer (2nd edn)
How to Study an E. M. Forster Novel
How to Study James Joyce
How to Study Linguistics (2nd edn)

How to Study Modern Poetry
How to Study a Novel (2nd edn)
How to Study a Poet (2nd edn)
How to Study a Renaissance Play
How to Study Romantic Poetry (2nd edn)
How to Study a Shakespeare Play (2nd
    edn)
How to Study Television
Practical Criticism

Studying the Built Environment

Marion Temple

First published 2004 by
PALGRAVE MACMILLAN
Houndmills, Basingstoke, Hampshire RG21 6XS and
175 Fifth Avenue, New York, N.Y. 10010
Companies and representatives throughout the world

PALGRAVE MACMILLAN is the global academic imprint of the Palgrave Macmillan division of St. Martin's Press, LLC and of Palgrave Macmillan Ltd. Macmillan® is a registered trademark in the United States, United Kingdom and other countries. Palgrave is a registered trademark in the European Union and other countries.

ISBN 0–333–96919–7 paperback

This book is printed on paper suitable for recycling and made from fully managed and sustained forest sources.

A catalogue record for this book is available from the British Library.

10 9 8 7 6 5 4 3 2 1
13 12 11 10 09 08 07 06 05 04

Printed in China

Contents

PART FOUR: STUDY AND PRACTICE

List of Tables

Acknowledgements

While I have considerable experience of the built environment and of education for the built environment, I do not claim to be an expert in all its facets. I am accordingly grateful to many colleagues and friends for discussion during the time that I was writing this book. Particular thanks are due to those colleagues who contributed the individual sections identified in the text in relation to their personal subject specialisms: Peter Dent, Mike Stubbs and Helena Webster, all of the School of the Built Environment at Oxford Brookes University, and Pat Turrell of the School of Environment and Development at Sheffield Hallam University.

I am grateful to Oxford Brookes University for providing the teaching, research and academic development opportunities that provided much of the stimulus for writing this book.

I am also grateful both to the anonymous referees who provided useful comments on the original proposal for this book and to the referee whose comments on an earlier version of parts of the text were insightful and extremely helpful.

Thanks are due to my publisher and her colleagues at Palgrave Macmillan, whose help and encouragement throughout the process of writing this book and preparing it for publication have been greatly appreciated.

Finally, I would like to express particular thanks to my husband for his continuing patience and support.

Notes on the Contributors

Peter Dent (*see* pp. 79–82)
Peter Dent is Head of the Department of Real Estate and Construction at Oxford Brookes University. He is a Fellow of the Royal Institution of Chartered Surveyors. His current research interests include international comparative studies of the role of real estate in the public sector.

Mike Stubbs (*see* pp. 70–76)
Mike Stubbs is a part-time Senior Lecturer in Planning in the Department of Real Estate and Construction at Oxford Brookes University and part-time Land Use Planning Adviser to the National Trust. He is joint author of Ratcliffe and Stubbs, *Urban Planning and Real Estate Development*, and has published widely on dispute resolution and planning appeals. His current research is on the role of heritage in delivering strategies of sustainable development.

Pat Turrell (*see* pp. 87–91)
Pat Turrell is joint subject leader for Building Surveying and Building Technology at Sheffield Hallam University. A chartered building surveyor for 22 years and Fellow of the Royal Institution of Chartered Surveyors, her current research interest is why so few women enter the built-environment professions. A member of the RICS Raising the Ratio Group, she is part of the European JIVE project, working to create change in the sector.

Helena Webster (*see* pp. 61–64)
Helena Webster is a Reader in Architecture in the Department of Architecture at Oxford Brookes University. She is the author of *Architecture without Rhetoric: The Work of Alison and Peter Smithson*, and has written extensively on architectural history and architectural education. Her current research interests include the socialisation dimension of architectural education and the pedagogy of the design studio.

1 Studying the built environment: an introduction

The built environment in the early years of the new century is a challenging and stimulating arena in which to work. Key issues such as sustainability affect us all. The multi-disciplinary nature of this and other major issues has been reflected in a resurgence of interest in the need for built-environment professionals to understand each others' sphere of interest and to work together to create a better built environment for the future. In addition, increasing globalisation and changes in the way we work are affecting both employers and those who work in the built environment.

The dynamics of the world of work and of the problems facing the built environment affect the approach of educationalists to its teaching. It is the context of these issues and changes in the built environment that has informed my own thinking about education in the built environment over recent years and acted as the springboard for writing this book. I hope it will prove useful and stimulating both to students studying the built environment and to their tutors.

▶ 1.1 Aim and rationale

This book aims to weave together the unifying themes and aspects of studying the built environment while allowing space for the development of distinctive aspects of the separate contributing subjects and professions.

The underpinning rationale is that the book is learner-centred, as explained in more detail below – designed to help both current and potential students in their study of the built environment.

1.1.1 Learner-centredness
The overarching purpose of this book is to inform and assist students *at both undergraduate and postgraduate level* (and so, where relevant, also to assist tutors), in particular to:

- become more effective, reflective and independent learners;
- develop those core study skills and competencies that contribute to successful study and professional practice;

- understand the purposes of learning about the built environment;
- understand and appreciate the different subject disciplines and specialisms that contribute to study of the built environment: their distinctiveness, their inter-relationships and their similarities;
- understand the inter-relationships between principles and practice; between knowledge and skills competencies;
- appreciate the role and nature of professional practice and the role of the professional institutes;
- appreciate and value the diversity within the built environment;
- choose/refine a path of study, among the contributing subject disciplines, that will enable them to build upon their personal enthusiasms and competencies.

This book is intended not to be a subject text but to complement individual subject texts. It should help to raise awareness of the context of the individual subject components that comprise study of the built environment. Professional education for the built environment is often relatively lengthy. Consequently it is not uncommon for students to redefine and refocus the precise direction of their education during their studies in order to maximise their interest and enhance their study portfolio. In addition, as professional practitioners in a changing world, individuals may well return to education at various stages in their career in order to redirect their skills and energies in the light of evolving employment circumstances – movement across the various built-environment professions is an increasing feature of contemporary practice. The book should also be of use and interest in this context.

1.1.2 Organisation and scope of the book
The main features of the organisation and scope of this book are as follows:

- There is an explanation of the individual component subject disciplines and related professions within the overarching framework of the built environment; the explanation being set in the context of topical issues and with respect to current learning and teaching experience.
- The author's generalist, broad-based approach provides objective coverage reinforced by specialist expert contributions on individual topics.
- There are four parts in the book: they look at themes and challenges; subjects and courses; studying, skills and assessment; and study and practice.
- The book focuses upon the subject disciplines of architecture, construction, planning, real estate and, to a lesser extent, surveying, while exploring how other relevant subjects relate to these core areas.

▶ 1.2 Structure and content: overview

This book is divided into four parts, which are designed to help the reader understand more easily how the book is structured and to navigate around it. Part One, 'Themes and Challenges', explains the diversity to be found within the ambit of the built environment, and introduces some of the contemporary issues that bind together these diverse components, making an interdisciplinary approach to studying the built environment both important and enriching. Part Two, 'Subjects and Courses', considers the programmes of study that are linked to these topics, indicating the nature of the curriculum and content associated with studying the built environment. Part Three, 'Studying, Skills and Assessment', moves from the content of programmes of study to the experience of studying the built environment, encompassing skills and assessment in addition to methods of delivery. Part Four, 'Study and Practice', recognises that one objective of study is to achieve professional employment in the built environment, and so the book concludes by discussing the relationships between academic study and professional practice.

1.2.1 Chapter 2: Connecting themes

This chapter explores some of the main themes that serve to integrate the different disciplines connected with the built environment and contribute to the richness of its interdisciplinary study and practice. These themes are design, planning, investment and management.

Design is central to the built environment: the chapter looks at its importance, at exactly what design is; at design for cities; at whether or not there is inherent tension between form and function; at the contribution of intelligent buildings; and at the cultural context for design.

The process (as distinct from the subject) of planning is the second connecting theme the chapter explores: it looks at the process of planning and the work of planners; at differing cultures; at environmental issues; and at the roles of the public and private sectors.

Consideration of investment and finance in the built environment leads to such questions as: Who invests, given the increasing globalisation of the market for capital? What should be the roles of the public and private sectors? Who develops the built environment and, importantly, what is developed and for whom?

The final theme, of management, is articulated through the different aspects of management that are especially pertinent to the built environment: the role played by marketing in presenting and influencing our image of the built environment.

1.2.2 Chapter 3: Contemporary challenges

This chapter considers selected contemporary issues that offer exciting challenges to those learning about and working within the built environment. The focus is upon sustainability; cities and urbanisation; and developing the built environment. In each case the nature of the challenge is explored in order to demonstrate how the individual subject disciplines contribute to our understanding and analysis of these key issues.

The main section of the chapter studies the challenges posed by the urban environment, not least so as to demonstrate the way in which sustainability acts as a strong thread interwoven with the other contemporary challenges faced by the built environment. The roles of the private and public sectors are developed in the context of the city, and further analysed in relation to the associated costs and benefits to society. The final section of the chapter looks at some examples of property development, including the effects of globalisation, to illustrate some of the key points from Part One.

1.2.3 Chapter 4: Curriculum and content

This chapter focuses upon curriculum and content in order to explain more precisely what the core subject disciplines are about. For each of architecture, building and construction, planning, real estate and surveying, the core focus of the subject is explained. For some of these subjects, specialist experts in their field have contributed their personal insight into their chosen subject.

The coverage of these core subjects is complemented by a briefer treatment of the related contextual subjects of economics, law, and management.

1.2.4 Chapter 5: Courses in the built environment

This chapter explains the wide range of courses available under the broad umbrella of the Built Environment. The differences between modular and other course structures are explained along with other key features of course provision at undergraduate, post-experience and postgraduate level. For those readers about to embark upon a course of study in the Built Environment, there is a section about choosing a course and a university. The relationship between university courses and future careers is also investigated in this chapter. Many readers will aspire to professional careers, and some, but not all, courses carry professional accreditation, so this important aspect of choosing a course of study is explained.

1.2.5 Chapter 6: Studying the curriculum

This chapter introduces those learning and teaching methods that are most commonly experienced in studying the built environment. The built environment is the laboratory in which we study, and so the importance of applied learning from work experience and projects is emphasised. The final section of the chapter deals with the dissertation study that accounts for a major element in many built-environment programmes, whether at undergraduate or postgraduate level.

1.2.6 Chapter 7: Learning skills and techniques

This chapter introduces the study skills that are needed in order to learn about the built environment. The opening section of the chapter introduces learning techniques for personal reflection, which can assist study.

The main part of the chapter explains those individual study skills and techniques for learning that students can expect to find most useful in learning about the built environment, including interdisciplinarity; problem solving; team work and research skills. In addition, the more generic skills of information and communications technology, written competencies, visual competencies, oral communication, and numeracy are also covered.

1.2.7 Chapter 8: Learning and assessment

Chapter 8 builds upon Chapter 7 in order to explain the ways in which learning skills can assist in preparation for assessment. The type and content of assessment will reflect the learning outcomes of a course of study. This chapter will therefore help students to understand better the relationship between the material studied and the way in which it is likely to be assessed. Assessment can take a wide variety of forms, from oral presentations, to formal drawings, to report writing. It can include individual work and sometimes group work in order to develop the team-work skills discussed in Chapter 7.

A section of this chapter is devoted to examination techniques, because unseen written examinations remain a core element of assessment for many disciplines, and especially for those academic courses of study linked to exemption from, or credit towards, professional examinations.

1.2.8 Chapter 9: Academic study and professional practice

This final chapter looks at the outcomes of students' learning and attainments within the framework of the competencies necessary for contemporary professional practice. The key question of how academic study connects to professional practice in the built environment is addressed. One section investigates the links between academic study, research skills (either undergraduate or postgraduate) and practice in the information economy of the new century. Final sections of the chapter consider the role of the professional bodies in the built environment, both in helping to ensure academic standards and in the lifelong learning of their professional members.

Overall, the book explains the nature of the distinctive student experience to be expected while learning about the built environment, with a particular focus upon inter- and multi-disciplinarity, the inter-relationships between principles and practice, and the importance of practitioner competencies. Many readers of this book will be, or intend to become, built-environment professionals. The book therefore discusses the distinctive features of educating professionals through partnership with practice; the role and purpose of professional bodies; and the usefulness of experiential learning and of continuing professional development.

▶ 1.3 Who should use this book?

The book will be useful to all future and current students of the built environment and their tutors.

For potential students there are sections directly about the choice of a course and the choice of a university. The book also offers a great deal of background information with respect to both current issues and education in the built environment. Dipping into the book and picking up this information should assist in the choice of which subject to study and also of how to prepare for study of the built environment.

Undergraduate students should find it very helpful as an aid to seeing the context for the content of their study, which can become lost in the pressure of study and assessment. It will also provide important guidance with respect to study skills and assessment, in addition to providing useful information to guide module choice when different subjects and teaching styles are available.

For those undertaking postgraduate courses, especially those who studied a different subject during their undergraduate studies, this book will offer a broader perspective within which to place their individual course specialism. This wider perspective will assist in understanding the nature and culture of the overall construction and property industry within which their chosen professional career fits.

In addition, the book will help to guide non-cognate students towards the particular study skills and competencies that they can expect to find most useful during their built-environment studies.

As well as students, it is hoped that tutors will find this book useful as a tool to enable students to learn more about the wider context of their specialist studies, in addition to the core skills and competencies that will enrich their learning experience. The book is no substitute for subject-based texts, but should provide a useful complement to these textbooks.

This book will also be of interest to those currently in full-time professional practice who wish, or need, to undertake a programme of continuing professional development (CPD). For these readers, the book may act as a valuable source of revision and reminder with respect to learning skills and how to undertake academic study. In addition, the book should help to remind the reader of the inter-relationships between academic study and practice, so assisting the reader in understanding and maximising the benefits from academic study within the context of current professional practice.

▶ 1.4 How to use this book

Some readers may choose to read this book from cover to cover and I hope that they will find it an enjoyable read, should they do so. However, readers are more likely to use the book as a point of reference and dip into it in order to read the section that is most pertinent to them at a particular time. After all, at one time you may be interested in finding background information to assist you in your selection of modules, while, at another time, advice upon how to prepare for examinations or to approach writing a long essay or dissertation may be vital! For this reason, in addition to the summaries at the beginning of each chapter, the list of contents and the index have been prepared to help you to find your way around the book quickly and easily so that it is an accessible and user-friendly reference book.

In whatever way you prefer to use this book, I hope that it will provide a valuable guide to your studies. Most important, I hope that it will help you to enjoy studying the built environment.

Part One
Themes and Challenges

2 Connecting themes

> *The built environment is concerned with buildings, their spatial environment and the people who inhabit that environment. Before looking in more detail at the main subject disciplines within the umbrella of the Built Environment, in the present chapter we consider aspects of the life cycle of a building – its development, planning, design, finance and management – and the societal framework within which it takes place.*

▶ 2.1 Integration and interdisciplinarity

In recent years, the benefit of a more integrative and collaborative approach between the different built-environment professions has been increasingly appreciated both to help specialists in the different professions to understand each other's viewpoint and, in practical terms, to facilitate their working together on team projects. For this reason, this early chapter of the book adopts an overarching approach that investigates some examples of integrative and interdisciplinary themes to illustrate the connections and linkages between the individual Built Environment subject disciplines.

Until relatively recently, a root cause of some of the problems within the property industry was the 'silo' approach to educating the different professional disciplines. Each discipline emphasised its distinctiveness and individuality: architects cherished their fine arts background and their creativity, largely ignoring the commercial pressures of finance and management. In contrast, surveyors concentrated upon understanding costs and measurement. This specialism within the education and training of future property professionals led to cultural divides and a lack of interprofessional understanding within the property industry. An underlying cultural adjustment was therefore essential to enable the different specialists to make a positive contribution to the contemporary challenges facing the built environment. As we shall see in Chapter 3, the greatest of these challenges are interdisciplinary. For example, a meaningful strategy for attaining greater sustainability in the built environment cannot be achieved by a single profession alone.

Members of the different built-environment professions identify and value the differences between the disciplines and their distinctive cultures. For example, the professional culture and expectations of surveying and real estate management are distinct from those of building/construction management and distinct again from those of architecture. As a result, some elements of the educational curriculum associated with these professions are discipline-specific. In this respect, education can strengthen multi-disciplinarity. The multi-disciplinary strands in education mean that divisions between different bodies of knowledge and professional skills are retained, reinforced and valued. The resultant well-defined identity for the individual professional disciplines is clearly a welcome counterpart to the strong, identifiable professional ethos and culture embodied in the role of the professional institutions. But how do we nurture and retain these differences without reinforcing them to the extent that the silo culture becomes too strong and acts as a barrier to progress?

The very nature of the underlying contemporary issues such as the environment, development or sustainability lend themselves to an interdisciplinary approach. Sustainability is a key issue for the built environment: its attainment is dependent upon collaborative partnerships and working across the individual professions. Aspects of the educational curriculum related to topics such as sustainability are transferable across individual subject areas and so contribute directly to the evolution of a more interdisciplinary and potentially interprofessional approach to the study of the built environment.

What exactly do we mean by 'interprofessional'? Investigation of interprofessional pedagogy and practice began primarily within the healthcare-related subjects and has only recently become a subject of academic study in relation to the built environment. A current research project focusing upon the built environment defines working interprofessionally as 'where a relationship exists between two or more professions with some notion of reciprocity'. The description of interprofessional education derived from this definition is 'a learning process in which different professionals learn from and about each other in order to develop collaborative practice' (FDTL, Better Together research project, www.bettertogether.ac.uk 2001). So, in summary, while work in the built environment frequently involves participation in a multiprofessional team composed of a range of professional practitioners such as architects, builders and planners, explicit investigation into the nature of collaborative working between these different professionals and the ways in which the benefits of such working practices might be maximised, is relatively new.

▶ 2.2 Property development and life cycle

Neither individual buildings, nor groupings of buildings, nor the built environment of which they form a part, have an infinite life. Over time, buildings, categories of buildings, and urban areas either wear out and become physically dilapidated or alternatively become economically or technologically obsolescent.

Consequently, new individual buildings and groups of buildings are developed. Whether the new building is a residential house or apartment block, a single shop or an area of commercial buildings, the property development process helps to illustrate the contribution of many of the Built Environment subjects. A project to develop a building or group of buildings will need to look at:

- *property development*: the value of the site and/or building(s), appraisal of the proposed development, availability of finance for development, future income likely to be generated;
- *planning*: the planning framework and, in the case of urban development, urban design;
- *economics*: the economic, social and demographic characteristics of the location and the surrounding area;
- *architecture*: design, drawings, relationship of buildings to the site;
- *construction*: the physical characteristics of the site and the availability of services such as water, drainage, electricity, and telecommunications;
- *construction/surveying*: construction methods and materials, contracts, procurement and cost control;
- *planning/construction*: environmental impact, site impact, energy use;
- *real estate management*: purchase or acquisition of the site and/or building(s), management of the building(s) and site, security, sale or disposal of the site and/or building(s).

The finite life of buildings, and the built environment that they constitute, has resulted in the concept of a 'life cycle' approach to individual buildings and to functionally coherent groups of buildings. In studying the built environment, we can therefore follow a building or group of buildings through its life cycle from the cradle to the grave. Indeed, such an approach can offer a helpful perspective to illuminate the inter relationships between the different property-related professions and their different involvements in, and impacts upon, the built environment.

The next sections of this chapter accordingly introduce aspects of the typical life cycle for a building in an urban environment, focusing upon the different roles of design, planning, investment and finance, and management.

The final section of the chapter then considers the societal framework within which the built environment develops.

▶ 2.3 Design

2.3.1 Why does design matter?

Good design of a new building or group of buildings can positively enhance the quality of an area, while poor design can detract from the local built environment. Even if the individual building is built for private use, its impact upon the surrounding streets, sightlines and space means that the building has an impact upon the wider public. For this reason, in most countries, it is accepted that built-environment design is legitimately a matter of public, as well as private, interest.

This is particularly the case because buildings, while for the most part not permanent features of the landscape, are not ephemeral. Current design therefore affects the environment within which future buildings are designed and constructed: a mistake in the present constrains the quality of future development, while a success in the present adds to the possibility of high-quality future development.

Good design is therefore of value because it improves the quality of the built environment now and improves the likelihood of a high-quality future built environment. It also enhances the general social wellbeing associated with good-quality public spaces. It may contribute to the sustainability of the development. In addition to these qualitative effects, good design can bring the quantitative benefit of attracting future finance and investment into an area, as we shall see in Chapter 3.

Poor design arises when new buildings are not to scale with their setting, adversely affecting light and space in the surrounding streets, and reducing sightlines. Or a new building may be out of keeping with its surroundings as a result of its style rather than its size: there are tensions between the use of local traditional styles and modern universal styles. The particular difficulty with poor design is similar to that noted earlier in relation to good design: buildings are not ephemeral and therefore today's poorly designed buildings will continue to blight tomorrow's landscape.

Good design should therefore be encouraged as being in the public interest, being of benefit to the built environment and also to the economy and society within which it lies.

2.3.2 Design and function

Accessibility is an important element of the functionality both of single buildings and of groups of buildings. Retail property needs to be readily accessible by both customers and suppliers, or the retailer is unlikely to find the shop profitable. Multiple retailers in search of new sites will put accessibility and visibility high on their list of criteria for site choice. As workplaces, they also need to be accessible to the labour force that they will employ.

Accessibility can be affected by the quantity and quality of access roads in the area, by street and building lighting and by the quality of signage both in the neighbourhood and on the building.

Accessibility also affects the functioning of the building once a person has entered it. Psychology has always played a role in architectural design, with respect to the form of the building but also with respect to features such as the use of colour and lighting within its interior. At the extreme, today's multiple retailers utilise psychology in many aspects of store design and layout in order to help to persuade customers to spend more time and money in their shops.

Issues of accessibility are more critical for the disabled, and many governments and governmental bodies, such as the European Union, have detailed legislation designed to ensure at least minimum rights of access. Compliance with such legislation affects the internal design of buildings, from the provision of adequate lighting and lifts to the provision of tactile surfaces and appropriate signage. Similar considerations affect the external environment, where signage and lighting can be as important as the removal of obstacles and provision of smooth gradients of pavements and kerbs.

Accessibility, both external and internal, is therefore just one example of the ways in which the building's future function will affect the design process.

2.3.3 Design and sustainability

Notions of passive design are central to the enhancement of sustainability within the built environment, and so immediately serve to connect the apparently disparate concepts of design and sustainability. Interestingly, the drive towards designing a more sustainable built environment inherently pushes the built-environment professions towards discourse because the attainment of greater sustainability requires a more holistic approach to designing the built environment. The traditional, compartmentalised approach of the mid-twentieth century will not yield a sustainable outcome. For example, in order to enhance sustainability within the design of buildings, the architect needs to understand, and to work alongside, the structural engineer, the electrical engineer and the specialist technologist.

Both design and materials can radically affect the thermal efficiency and ventilation of a building. Our current understanding of these relationships means that the design of the building as a visually attractive form is no longer independent of the technical performance of the building as a structure.

► 2.4 Planning

The planning process is the second connecting theme to be explored in relation to the building life cycle, looking at the process of planning and the work of planners; at the roles of the public and private sectors; and at such ideas as consensus planning.

2.4.1 Private interest and the public interest

We noted above that the design of the built environment becomes a matter for the public interest because the design impact of an individual building, or of a group of related buildings, influences the space surrounding it and therefore affects us all as users of that space. The role of planning is to mediate between private preference and public interest within the context of the design, development and use of the built environment.

The detail of the planning framework varies over time and between different countries, but many of the underlying principles are generic. Land is a scarce resource, especially land in popular urban locations, and so it has to be rationed and its use controlled. The need to control use in the face of competing uses underpins the evolution of the development plan, or planned zones allocated to different activities. Planners design plans in the light of known current and anticipated future demand. Then they control the actual development that takes place within the framework of the development plan.

Planning therefore involves judgements. Does the proposed building fit into the current development plan for the area in terms of land use and economic activity? Is its scale appropriate to the surrounding built environment? Is its design in keeping with its surroundings?

Planning can act as a positive influence upon the design of the built environment by encouraging good design and by rejecting poor design. In this way planning serves the public interest by enhancing environmental quality. The public interest should also inform the development plan for an area. How planners interpret the public interest in this context varies. In some cases, the planner or the government may act as sole arbiter of the public interest and impose plans without consultation with the wider public. At the other extreme, a putative development plan may be the subject of a widespread consultation process involving the public in general and also the public as represented by various interest groups such as residents, employers and amenity associations.

Once a development plan is in place, the role of the planner is to interpret the plan. A proposal to build that fits within the plan should therefore be acceptable, as the planner is enforcing the plan as distinct from exercising judgment based upon personal taste. Planning should not be arbitrary and unpredictable: plans should be communicable and predictable, resulting in consistent decision-making with respect to proposals to build.

The application of a current development plan provides the information that serves as the basis for the future revised development plan. Planning therefore involves a dynamic process of iteration and feedback in response to the dynamics of change in the built environment and its use by the public.

To illustrate these underlying principles with a practical example, let us look at the case where a property developer is proposing to develop a single-storey development comprising ten retail shop units on the edge of a small town. The town has existed for many centuries and has an old religious building of local, historical, vernacular architectural interest in its central district. The developer anticipates that the new shops will attract a mixture of general, food and clothes stores as future tenants.

Will the local planners welcome such a proposal?

The answer will largely depend upon the relationship of the proposal to the planning guidance for the locality. Is the proposal consistent with any guidance or policies respecting the urban development and/or redevelopment of this historic town? Does the local plan zone this location for retail development? Where it exists, is such zoning designed to encourage solely retail developments, or is there an expressed preference for mixed-use buildings? Mixed use is seen as important where planning authorities aim for more sustainable communities: communities in which people can live, work and play without the need to travel between different locations. In many planning regimes, this proposal could be improved by the relatively simple expedient of altering it to a two-storey development, offering residential accommodation above the shops.

We have not yet considered the visual nor the environmental impact of the building. What materials are proposed for the new development? Are they in harmony with the existing local character and architecture of the town? What type and quality of building materials are proposed? Are these visually attractive? Do they contribute to the longer-term goals of enhanced sustainability and environmental efficiency? Is the proposed new range of shops accessible? Can potential customers reach and move around it safely and comfortably? Can suppliers deliver to the building safely and easily without impeding existing patterns of transport and movement in the vicinity?

This discussion has outlined the type of features that planners would wish to consider before deciding whether or not to permit the developer to build. These considerations will determine whether or not the development proceeds in relation to planning guidance. In addition, however, the developer will only proceed if there is a perceived demand for the buildings – in this case, a development of retail units – from potential buyers.

Commercial property, and to a lesser extent residential property, will be bought by two distinct categories of purchaser. First, there are the owner-occupiers, who purchase a building in order to use it for their own benefit.

Secondly, there is the investor, who purchases the building in order to max-imise the value that can be earned from it through letting it to tenants, and then future resale.

Retail owners will assess the relative merits of a possible retail purchase by weighing up the expected economic costs and benefits. The benefits from the acquisition can be estimated from consideration of the likely future revenue stream to be earned from sales generated from the proposed shop. Revenue will come from customers and therefore depends upon demand. This in turn will depend upon the characteristics of the local area, such as population, wealth and density, and the attractiveness and accessibility of the retail development compared with other shopping destinations in the area. The presence or otherwise of competitors in the vicinity will also be important. The costs will be direct costs such as rent, heating and security, but also costs associated with the ease of delivery and storage of stock.

The above considerations all relate to the retail development as an oper-ational asset, designed for use. Investors will be interested in these opera-tional aspects, because they will affect the attractiveness of the development to future tenants and so influence the level of rent that can be charged. Investors will also be interested in whether the location in general appears to be improving or deteriorating in quality, and whether or not the develop-ment and its vicinity may have future potential for redevelopment when the current buildings become old or obsolete. These considerations affect the value of property as an investment asset and are linked to the financing of the built environment – a topic to which we shall return in the next section of this chapter.

We have travelled some distance from our initial introduction of the idea of planning, as it has led us to introduce the concepts of the development and then the use of buildings in addition to the original planning phase of the property life cycle. This is why planning and economic development are so closely related. Buildings are used – and used by people – and so we can extend the relationship from planning to economics and to sociology. Healey (1997) sought to draw together the contributions of economics and sociol-ogy to planning, and to investigate how the different stakeholders in a place could best cooperate in order to maximise the benefit of their contribution to that place.

As part of her analysis, she investigates the added value that the resources located there bring to a location. Her concept of the institutional capacity of a place attempts to capture *'an embodiment of the relational resources avail-able in the social networks of a place'* (Healey, 1997, p. 140). This is much more diverse and inherently richer than the simpler approach to economic development of considering the contribution made by local employment to the local economy. Healey's approach considers the quality of the local labour force, that is, its educational qualifications, skills and attributes, as well as the quantity of the labour force. The relationship of employing organisations to the infrastructure is also considered, for example in relation to their impact upon transport and roads; their demand for utilities such as water; and the nature of their impact upon environmental quality.

The role of planning and the planner from Healey's perspective helps us to distinguish clearly between planning and urban design. The role of planning within urban design is reflected in LeGates observation that 'the planner's defining goal is no longer merely to impose order on nature, but to continuously impose order on the city itself' (LeGates, in LeGates and Stout, 1996). This perspective emphasises the contribution of planners to the design of the model city, while Healey's perspective emphasises the contribution of planners to the social sciences.

▶ 2.5 Investment and finance

2.5.1 Financing the built environment

Here we are interested in the general principles of finance and their application to the built environment. Whether you want to buy a house or are interested in how a major urban redevelopment would be financed, knowledge of the variety of different funding sources available and their relative merits is essential. The size of purchase inherent in the acquisition of any form of building is such that it is normally necessary to borrow money in order to fund the acquisition. It is realistic to envisage the repayment of this loan over a relatively long period because buildings survive for the long term. For this reason, one crucial aspect of financing purchases in the context of the built environment concerns the timescale over which it is best to borrow funds and the differing rates of interest that apply to those different timescales. If the project is a large one, such as a major office development, then the anticipated timescale for the receipt of sale revenue or rental income will also be an important consideration. These factors are reflected in consideration of the influence upon cash flows over time, associated with different funding sources. Because buildings survive for the long term, the sale value or rental income value associated with the building in the future is important. Because these refer to future dates, considerations of uncertainty and risk are pertinent, further complicating analysis of efficient financing for the built environment.

An additional dimension has become increasingly relevant in recent decades, and this is the globalisation of finance. The larger financial institutions, such as banks and insurance companies, are truly international companies operating on a multinational basis. This has affected the level of interest rates, which are increasingly determined in an effectively international market. It also affects the availability of finance in different locations as these institutions calculate the risk associated with different types of building and also different places in which to invest their money (Temple, 1994, pp. 41–6, pp. 170–2).

2.5.2 Investment in real estate

With respect to investment in real estate, it is important to distinguish commercial real estate, such as factories, shops and offices, from residential real estate.

Commercial real estate is a relatively specialised investment vehicle. Its specialist nature arises for three main reasons. First, commercial real estate is often 'lumpy' as an investment. That is to say, buildings are large and valuable assets and so require a significant capital sum in order to finance their acquisition. In technical terms, real estate is indivisible as an investment vehicle, which means that it cannot easily be reduced to small quantities, although some recent specialist financial vehicles attempt to overcome this characteristic. Secondly, commercial real estate is relatively illiquid because its market price tends to fluctuate over time rather than remaining stable. When prices fluctuate downwards, it is difficult to sell real estate without incurring a loss on the capital value of the asset. The time to sell is therefore constrained – hence the illiquidity of real estate. Thirdly, ownership of commercial real estate brings with it responsibilities for its management. Real estate management is in itself a management specialism. Therefore, investors may prefer not to become involved in the acquisition of real estate unless they have access to specialist management support.

The specialist nature of commercial real estate has encouraged the growth of specialist providers in recent decades. For example, during the 1990s, the concept of selling retail real estate to a specialist real estate holding company and leasing it back to the occupier for their use became increasingly common practice for large organisations, in particular in the USA and UK. More recently, some of the major hotel chains, often with global coverage and property ownership, have been undertaking similar 'sale and leaseback' arrangements with specialist real estate organisations.

One important element in investment in real estate is the part played by the financial institutions. For example, pension funds often hold a proportion of their investments either directly in real estate or indirectly through real estate investment vehicles. For financial institutions such as pension funds, property becomes another class of asset in which to invest. It is a useful asset category because cyclical variations in the return on real estate investment tend to be different over time from variations in the return on equities and government fixed interest bonds. Real estate therefore allows the institutional investors to further diversify their portfolios and spread risk.

However, real estate itself can be quite illiquid – as explained above – and quite risky. Different categories of real estate tend to alter in value differentially over time, as do different locations. So, for example, over a ten-year period, office property may prove a more profitable investment than retail property; or investment in property in Frankfurt may be more profitable than investment in the London property market. For these reasons, a number of more sophisticated real estate investment vehicles have been developed which essentially allow the investor to invest in real estate assets but to do so indirectly rather than directly, so that their investment can be spread across different classes of property and different locations, so helping to spread risk and reduce variability in the rate of return achieved.

Residential real estate does not necessarily involve characteristics of indivisibility and specialist management requirements to a similar extent – although liquidity issues associated with price fluctuations over time do apply equally. Large owners of residential real estate, such as local government, may in some countries make arrangements for specialist management of their properties analogous to those outlined above for commercial real estate. The same may be true of large landlords who own a sizeable portfolio of residential properties. Because the size and value of a single house is typically less than the size and value of a factory or office, private small investors are more likely to invest in residential than in commercial real estate. In countries such as the UK, with a growing proportion of households buying and owning their own homes, the number of very small investors in residential property is increasing through the process of home ownership.

Traditionally, when people were less geographically mobile and typically continued to live in the district of their birth, houses, once owned, would be passed down from one generation to the next with no financial transaction occurring. Increasing mobility has brought market transactions further into the housing market because the following generation will not necessarily wish to inhabit the same district as their parents. This in itself has implications for the financing required to support such ownership – which will be very different from the financing required to underpin large-scale investment in commercial real estate portfolios.

▶ 2.6 Management

The theme of management in relation to buildings and the built environment is briefly introduced here through the different aspects of management that are especially pertinent to the built environment: facilities management; project management and real estate management.

'Facilities management' refers to the management of the facilities within and around buildings and groups of buildings. It can encompass responsibility for the lighting on an office development or business park to the provision of replacement light bulbs; responsibility for the security of an entire development, to responsibility for the replacement of an individual lock.

Facilities management is therefore related to both construction management and real estate management. 'Real estate management' can focus upon the operational, day-to-day use of property, either in relation to a specific building or building group or in relation to the property utilised by a large company such as a multiple retailer. A further aspect is the management of the real estate components of an investment portfolio held by a business, or a financial organisation such as a banking or insurance company.

'Project management' is associated with the implementation of built-environment projects, including the initial development, construction and use of buildings. It therefore provides an overarching connection between the different phases of development, design, planning, finance, construction and management of the built environment. (In practice, project management is often an important component of the construction management curriculum and, for this reason, project management is discussed in further detail in the relevant section of Chapter 4.)

Specific aspects of management practice are relevant to all of these areas of management of the built environment. For example, during the past decade the use and application of information technology to management systems has altered the practice of property management from facilities management to real estate investment management. As a further example, many companies value the role played by marketing in presenting and influencing their image and the branding in terms of their use of the built environment.

This brief introduction to the role of management as a theme across the built environment is followed up by further consideration, in Chapter 4, of management as a subject taught in the Built Environment curriculum, and in Chapter 7 where the specific attributes of management as a desirable skill to be gained from studying the built environment are discussed.

▶ 2.7 The societal framework

Buildings are inhabited by people and serve a social function: the study of the built environment therefore exists within its society. Consequently, the social sciences play an important part in informing the theory and context for studying the built environment. For example, architects study social culture in order to understand better the context for the architectural design of buildings at different times and places. Students of real estate study economic theory to elucidate the behaviour of people in market situations, the ways in which these vary over time and space, and the nature of their impact upon the market for real estate assets. Planners study sociology in order to understand the behaviour patterns of people in their daily lives at home and at work. Planning is also affected by the socio-political framework: the context of planning the built environment will be very different in a society with little government intervention in private-sector decisions as compared with a society with an active government that seeks to regulate the location and development of the built environment.

Society is not static but dynamic, and so changes that have an effect upon society and people's behaviour and decision making will also affect their demands of the built environment. The information technology revolution has hastened globalisation by encouraging firms to extend their supply chains and labour force across continents, with resulting changes in location and in building requirements. Information technology has changed the nature and content of many jobs, so affecting both people's working practices and their workplace requirements.

The expansion of jobs requiring creative skills has led to a reassessment of the design and layout of workplaces intended to foster cooperation and creativity amongst groups of workers. More generally, the acknowledgement that productivity can be significantly affected by the workplace has led to greater analysis of how employees behave at work, and of what constitutes 'good design' in this socio-economic context.

Economics and sociology also help students of the built environment to understand the rationale for, and the nature of, economic and social changes that affect people's activities and therefore their consequent use of buildings. As economies develop, production and employment typically shift from agriculture, to manufacturing, and then services, both for consumers and for producers. These shifts are associated with changes in the organisation and location of production and employment that affect the built environment. For example, in the many economies today facing a movement of population away from agriculture and rural areas in search of more remunerative employment in the city, there are the consequent pressures deriving from rapid urbanisation. Economies experiencing a shift away from manufacturing to services, then, typically find that the traditional preferred urban locations of manufacturing industry cease to be attractive to the service providers, leading to problems of urban dereliction and the need for urban regeneration.

Sociology also contributes to our understanding of people's lifestyles and preferences for the use of their time away from the workplace. Understanding of community and place is an essential foundation for effective planning and urban design. Those interested in real estate are also interested in understanding the influences upon lifestyle that will affect demand for a wide variety of real estate, from the preferred size of residential housing to demand for retail provision. For example, do shoppers prefer a range of small stores from which to choose or would they prefer the convenience of fewer larger retail outlets?

As soon as we begin to consider people's lifestyle and behaviour, both within and outside the workplace, then psychology also becomes part of the broader context. Architects are interested in psychology in order to understand how people respond to architectural design, colour, shape and space. The psychology of our response to space affects workplace design, as mentioned above, but also the interior design of spaces where we spend leisure time, from shopping to eating.

This section should have demonstrated the extent to which the study of the built environment is grounded in the study of society and therefore some of the ways in which it draws upon the theoretical framework of the social and behavioural sciences in order to understand people's interplay with the buildings and spaces in which they work and live.

▶ 2.8 Connections within the built environment

While this chapter has introduced some very different subjects, ranging from design, to planning, to finance, there are connections that serve to glue together the subject disciplines relating to the built environment. All these highly diverse subjects contribute towards the education of professional practitioners with a shared interest in enhancing the built environment. In studying the built environment, the connections with professional practice are therefore important, and will be discussed more fully in later sections of the book.

In studying the built environment, you will find that some research is strongly practice-oriented while other research is more theoretical. The research ethos that informs the curriculum in planning and management is different from that which informs the architecture curriculum. The latter is more heavily practice-based, and arguably, much valuable reflective practice that takes place within architecture is not actively extended into a research framework.

The earlier sections of this chapter have demonstrated some of the connecting themes within the built environment. There are very different cultures and concerns within each of the subjects that contribute to a holistic view of the built environment, and this inherent variety forms part of the richness to be found in studying it. One pedagogic research project

> yielded a rich matrix of practice, the discipline specific being interwoven with the interdisciplinary. This indicates a real strength for the property

professions and their development once a balance between an individual culture, such as that of surveying, and an understanding of the wider inter-disciplinary property context can be attained. (Temple, 2002, chapter 8, section 7.1)

In studying the built environment, you should seek to find your own balance between the interdisciplinary and your single disciplinary specialism.

3 Contemporary challenges

This chapter introduces sustainability as a unifying challenge faced by the contemporary built environment. The main section of the chapter considers sustainability in the context of cities and urbanisation, where issues pertinent to the different subject disciplines, considered in more detail in Chapter 4, are introduced.

▶ 3.1 Sustainability

The example of global warming and the effects of the consequential climate change upon the built environment serve as a potent example of the linkages between the natural environment and the built environment. The linkage between the natural environment and the built environment is paralleled by that between the natural form and the built form. The identity of the region and of the locality is intertwined with its natural environment: consequently an apt built environment will retain local built forms and value traditional land use and materials. Promotion of regional identity and regional characteristics will result in a built environment well adapted to the natural environment of the region.

Global standardisation of the built environment will result in poorly adapted buildings unsuited to the regional climate and environmental conditions. For example, the ancient temples at Oaxaca in Mexico were built to withstand disturbance by the earthquakes that were, and are, a typical occurrence of the region and these stone structures have consequently survived for centuries. Buildings constructed by modern, standard methods during the last century proved not to be proof against earthquake tremors.

Traditional construction techniques and siting designed to ensure effective drainage and make the most of natural protection from the elements provide less dramatic examples of the benefits of local knowledge embedded in the built environment. Difficulties of drainage and flooding are widespread today in many countries where the lessons of the past and local knowledge have been ignored in favour of the ill-thought application of inter-nationally standard building and development patterns.

A harmonious marriage between the natural environment and the built environment is one necessary condition for the attainment of sustainability: a central challenge for the contemporary built environment. According to the landmark definition contained in the 1987 Brundtland Report, 'Sustainable development is development that meets the needs of the present without compromising the ability of future generations to meet their own needs' (United Nations World Commission, 1987).

Sustainable development seeks to:

* conserve both the quantity and quality of natural resources such as water;
* protect the planet's biodiversity through protecting natural habitats;
* reduce the use of fossil fuels through, for example, the construction of 'green' energy-efficient buildings, and the design of low-energy transport systems;
* encourage mixed-use development of the built environment so that work and leisure activities are not highly spatially separated: a separation that again adds to fuel usage and travel.

The concept of sustainability and the inherent interlinkages between build-ings, the materials of which they are constructed, and the users of those buildings mean that built-environment professionals work together – and also work together with other professional practitioners such as engineers and economists. Urban design and urban regeneration are key examples of projects and problems demanding input from a range of professionals. In the UK, the Urban Task Force Report published in 1999 recognised the strong interconnections between the social benefits of a high-quality urban envi-ronment and the attainment of sustainability in order to safeguard the quality of the environment into the future.

Sustainable development considers the environmental impact of the eco-nomic activities conducted in buildings and in cities. This environmental impact will feed through into an effect upon the future social value of the local built environment. A blinkered view and short-termism are the antithe-ses of sustainability. If individuals and society can be encouraged to take a broader and longer view and to think about society and its future, then every-one will benefit, yielding a more sustainable built and natural environment.

To illustrate just a few aspects of the considerable challenge posed by the desirability of achieving sustainable development, this first section of the chapter now looks at three very different examples. These three examples are drawn from building, planning, and the economics of real estate, although all three examples have wider applicability across the other Built Environment subjects.

3.1.1 Sustainable development: How do we build?

In the opening paragraphs of this chapter, it was stated that sustainable development seeks to 'reduce the use of fossil fuels through, for example, the construction of "green" energy-efficient buildings'. Accordingly we now investigate more precisely what is meant by a 'green' building, and how it might be achieved, not only in the case of landmark buildings but also more generally in the construction of buildings.

It is in the interests of sustainability for buildings to have a low, rather than a high, environmental impact. Some building materials and components are more environmentally friendly than others: the challenge is to encourage those taking the relevant construction decisions to utilise materials, components and designs with a relatively low environmental impact.

Energy-efficient building begins with the design process so that the architecture is sympathetic to the local conditions both of the climate and also of the exact orientation and layout of the site. By taking account of such factors as north/south orientation and prevalent wind directions, the building design can reduce future energy requirements for internal heating and cooling. Paying attention to the intended pattern of use of the finished building will inform design for air circulation and ventilation, which can also be designed to complement the energy efficiency of the overall design. It has been demonstrated that energy-efficient design utilised in conjunction with appropriate building materials can minimise the heating and cooling requirements for commercial and residential buildings in a country with a climate such as that of the UK.

It is relatively easy to achieve the construction of a limited number of landmark sustainable buildings on high-profile sites, but how can the principles of sustainability be embedded into the design and construction process so that they can be readily adopted more widely by the construction industry?

One approach to answering this question is offered by guidance manuals such as *The Green Guide to Specification* (Anderson, Shiers and Sinclair, 2002). These guidance manuals are intended to enable those architects, surveyors, construction managers and owners seeking to reduce the environmental impacts of building materials to make informed choices. The guidance aims to provide clear information as to whether the materials and components that are being specified for a building have a low or high environmental impact. For example, the *Green Guide*'s environmental profiling system offers guidance for designers, property owners and facilities managers on the relative environmental impact of over 250 building materials and components. The environmental ratings in the *Green Guide* provide a reliable and straightforward way for designers and specifiers to base their choices on carefully researched, quantitative data. The system is designed to be easy for busy professionals to use in their day-to-day management of building projects. Building materials with a low environmental impact can be selected for construction and refurbishment projects, using a straightforward 'A B C' rating system. Guidance is comprehensive, covering specification options for all the principal building elements including external and internal walls, floor systems and finishes, paints, insulation and landscaping.

The *Green Guide* environmental profiling system was designed by staff in the Department of Real Estate and Construction at Oxford Brookes University, in collaboration with a commercial profit-making organisation and in partnership with the Building Research Establishment. It therefore offers one example of the benefits to be obtained through collaboration among the private sector, academic and research institutions. In addition to being multi-sector and multi-institutional, the project team was multi-disciplinary. This enabled a wide-ranging approach to be taken to this aspect of the important interdisciplinary issue of sustainability in construction, to the benefit of a number of the built-environment professions.

As well as the initial design and construction process, the longevity of the building can affect its sustainability. If a building is 'right first time' then it may well last for the duration of its projected lifespan, hence contributing towards the goal of sustainability. This can be seen more clearly when it is contrasted with the opposite possibility: where the property is not 'right first time', early obsolescence is more likely. Early obsolescence will require the early death of the property, making it more likely that the process of renewal begins rapidly relative to the possible lifespan of the original building. Such early renewal creates more demand for construction materials, and for the energy used during the construction process, and so is relatively unsustainable.

A variety of facets can contribute to the premature obsolescence of a property: it may become technologically obsolete, for example, through changes in the occupier's information technology requirements. A property may become functionally obsolete: there would cease to be much demand for petrol stations if cars ceased to be a preferred means of transport or were no longer fuelled by petrol. A property may become geographically obsolete if its location ceases to be attractive and/or relevant: there has been an over-supply of redundant warehouse building adjacent to docks in locations where the mode of transport for heavy and bulky freight has changed from sea shipment to air and rail shipment.

For all of these reasons, buildings, groups of buildings, and sometimes whole towns and cities can become obsolescent and redundant. When this happens, the challenge of sustainability is often to encourage successful redevelopment and regeneration. In addition to the renewal of the physical buildings, successful regeneration requires a rebuilding of confidence in the location. In practice, the latter often also proves to be a significant challenge.

Whether or not a building or a group of buildings last for their projected lifespan or meet a premature end depends upon a subtle blend of the contributory aspects to the built environment: upon a combination of design, planning, investment and management. Re-use and redevelopment also depend upon socio-economic influences such as confidence, in addition to the quality of buildings and design. Again, it is not one professional discipline alone but an interdisciplinary approach that is necessary for the successful attainment of this aspect of sustainability.

3.1.2 Sustainable development: Where do we build?

In the opening section of this chapter, it was stated that sustainable development seeks to 'encourage mixed-use development of the built environment so that work and leisure activities are not highly spatially separated: a separation that again adds to fuel usage and travel'.

Planners are in favour of mixed-use development that locates employment close to housing and leisure activities so as to minimise people's routine travel needs. In the mature industrial economies, real estate developers have responded to the increased private car usage of recent decades, combined with the deterioration in the quality of the built environment in many urban centres, by developing on out-of-town sites.

In the UK, the tensions between the town centre locations favoured by planners and the out-of-town locations favoured by real estate developers were highlighted by the development of huge out-of-town retail centres, many of which serve a sub-regional catchment area attracting shoppers from long distances by providing extensive free car parking and a comfortable, modern shopping experience. As well as generating more traffic, these out-of-town retail centres have been accused of contributing to the loss of retail trade and further retail decline in city centres. As a result, the UK government eventually sought to halt all sizeable out-of-town retail development in the interests of the sustainable development of urban centres.

In spite of the planners' preference for city centre activity, it has proved more difficult to prevent at least a proportion of newly created employment from going to out-of-town locations. One important reason for this trend is the development of the business park as an employment location, often not developed in conjunction with housing provision.

In the UK in the late 1980s, the government amended the planning framework so as to allow the development of new space designed for commercial office and light industrial use on greenfield as well as brownfield sites. It was this planning change that saw the birth of the business park – a concept that has also proved popular in North America and Western Europe.

Proponents argue that the business park creates the ideal working environment: a highly accessible, high-quality workspace generating high employee productivity combined with the agglomeration economies created by networking and support service provision within the boundaries of the business park. Opponents argue that the business park is not sustainable: it drains resources from traditional urban locations and encourages journeys over longer distances, and more journeys by car.

The distinctive features of most business parks can be summarised as:

- provision of commercial space, primarily for office and light industrial use;
- proactive management of the site and its component buildings, services and facilities, usually including active marketing;
- accessible location, usually with good road transport links for suppliers, customers and the workforce;
- low-density development with a unified site design, usually including landscaping and provision of complementary services, such as facilities for recreational sports, as well as extensive car parking.

Business parks therefore typically attract high-value businesses, creating employment that is often at a distance from housing provision and with extensive car parks compared with in-town sites. Most business parks have not contributed to the provision of locations for expanding small local businesses: instead many have aimed to attract prominent companies with a high added value in order to match their aspiration for market placement and an image as clean, high-quality entities. The search for an image of quality combined with the relatively low density of development means that business parks tend to be relatively costly locations. In addition, their concept of low-density development is usually incompatible with city centre locations with higher land values. In spite of the planners' expressed preferences for in-town locations for employment, business parks have typically developed out of town, so adding to the debate as to their desirability in relation to the sustainability agenda. This issue is explored further in section 3.2 of this chapter, in relation to the provision of housing, transport and employment within cities.

3.1.3 Sustainable development: What price the environment?
In the opening section of this chapter, it was stated that sustainable development seeks to 'conserve both the quantity and quality of natural resources such as water'; and to 'protect the planet's bio-diversity through protecting natural habitats'.

Economists base the price of goods upon the preferences of individual buyers and sellers as expressed through the operation of a perfectly functioning market. In real estate, the value of property is measured similarly. However, there are some important issues associated with the measure of value and prices in the built environment:

- How do we put a price upon the value of those goods and attributes that are not readily bought and sold in the marketplace?
- How do we put a price upon the positive amenity value of good urban design?
- How do we put a price upon the positive amenity value of a landscape?
- How do we put a price upon the negative cost of a landscape scarred by quarrying or mining?
- How do we put a price upon the negative cost of cleaning up a contaminated site in order to redevelop it?

In economics, prices are determined by the interaction of buyers and sellers through the medium of the market. For the market to function effectively, four basic conditions must be met:

- The products must be identical – that is, if one kilo of rice is the same as the next kilo of rice, buyers do not mind which kilo of rice they buy;
- Buyers and sellers must have perfect information so that they know the price that a kilo of rice is selling for, and are certain of that price;
- There must be a large number of people buying rice and a large number of sellers of rice;
- There must be no myopia, that is, people should not overlook the future effects of their current buying and selling actions.

As soon as we look at the built environment, we can see that there are problems in meeting these stringent conditions:

- Even if the physical buildings – whether houses, shops or offices – are identical, they will be differentiated in the eyes of potential buyers and sellers by characteristics associated with their location or their building specification.
- Information is less than perfect: there are costs of searching for information; some property market information is confidential and therefore inaccessible; and there is uncertainty with respect to future market information.
- There may be a large number of buyers and sellers, for example, in a smoothly working residential real estate market. However, the role of the

public sector and that of large organisations as buyers and sellers of property limit this.

• There is myopia – people skew their decisions towards the present. (The riskiness of the future ensures that this myopia continues even where techniques such as Discounted Cash Flow are utilised to counteract it.)

The subject disciplines of real estate valuation, economic development and planning are evolving techniques for placing a price or value upon non-traded goods and attributes such as those referred to above, but these techniques remain imperfect. Techniques such as hedonic pricing seek to place a value upon the attributes of a product but these techniques continue to assume that the market operates in perfect conditions. Alternative approaches, such as contingent valuation, begin from goods that are traded in the market in order to establish a value for those goods that cannot be easily traded through the market. However, these techniques are too data hungry to be widely applicable.

These measurement issues are important to students of the built environment because all real estate and buildings have environmental attributes, such as their location and their aesthetic design, that cannot be readily measured. The price of real estate – typically its value on the open market – assumes that the market is operating efficiently, while in practice such efficiency is rare. Techniques so far developed by real estate valuation have also proved somewhat asymmetric: there is more emphasis upon the measurement of social costs, such as those associated with site contamination, than there is upon the measurement of social benefit, such as that derived from the retention and provision of open spaces and good urban design.

In summary, while it is not impossible, it has proved difficult to adapt market prices to reflect the objective of sustainable development. This difficulty includes attempts to put a price onto the benefits of conserving the natural resources and habitats referred to at the beginning of this section.

The three very different examples in section 3.1, drawn from different subject areas, illustrate the diversity of the challenges posed by sustainable development. In practice, most buildings and people are located in cities and therefore the main part of this chapter discusses sustainability in the context of aspects of the city and the urban environment.

▶ 3.2 Cities and urbanisation

3.2.1 Concepts of Utopia: architecture and planning
The attainment of Utopia in the city is complicated by issues such as the difficulties and questionable desirability of building on greenfield sites and

building entirely new cities. More frequently, existing urban sites are redeveloped, with consequent problems associated with their contamination through previous use.

Utopian visions often envisage mixed-use development within which housing, employment, education, health, shopping and leisure facilities are all conveniently located within the same neighbourhood so as to minimise the need to travel. For example, 'a growing proportion of residents will work in the neighbourhood in which they live' (DETR, 1998b, p. 65). This UK Department of the Environment, Transport and the Regions Report envisages this objective as being attainable through the tool of proactive urban design, with urban design acting as the driver for change in the composition of the city through the process of urban regeneration. The Report was very design focused, articulating the view that 'the principles of design excellence, social well being and legislative framework' could be harnessed in order to provide a significant improvement in the quality of life for the vast majority of the population who are city dwellers.

This vision was further articulated in the concept of the compact city, described for example by Rogers and Power in *Cities for a Small Country* (2000). In their vision, the compact city has the benefits of high density and diversity that engender an energetic, exciting and vibrant living community. The compact city has the benefit of convenience through close proximity. When it functions well, the dynamics of a compact city could act as a positive glue for a fragmented society. Political leadership in the city could provide the environment in which good urban design can help to integrate communities and encourage a community spirit centred on shared citizenship. In Rogers and Power's urban Utopia, people actively want both to live and to work in the compact city.

How does the concept of the compact city relate to the observed cities of the world that are extensive – and usually expanding – conurbations? The conurbation, or meta-city, is far from compact but extends across a large space, encompassing a number of urban areas. One approach is to treat each of the core urban clusters within the conurbation as a compact city in its own right, so that the conurbation can be viewed as an urban web consisting of cities connected by transport routes. The urban design and planning challenge, then, is to focus sustainable development within each of the individual cities so as to minimise inter-city transport movements across the conurbation. In many cases, a central difficulty in the achievement of such an objective is that the pattern of local government fails to map onto the pattern of urban development. Where there is a single local governmental authority overseeing the entire conurbation, then its future development can be planned holistically. Where the conurbation is divided into a number of municipal districts, then such a holistic approach becomes more difficult and the different component cities within the conurbation may compete rather than cooperate, to the detriment of the overall sustainable development of the meta-city.

There are a number of practical obstacles in the path of attaining an urban Utopia, not least of which are economic considerations, often omitted from the urban designer's dream. A thriving urban society is dependent upon a thriving employment base in order to generate income and to attract both employers and employees into the city. In many post-industrial contemporary societies this is further complicated by people's preference for not living and working in the same location. In many cities, this preference is substantially cost driven – city centres are expensive and the cost of housing in a city centre location is often too high for most members of the workforce. In addition, there is evidence that people sometimes actively prefer a geographic separation of their work from their leisure (see, for example, Turok and Edge, 1999). In households with more than one earner, it is also often the case that the different individuals work at different locations, again making it less likely that employment and housing will be co-located.

In practice, much of the built fabric of a city is generated by real estate developers, who develop property in order to make a profit. Can the profit motive be reconciled with a Utopian vision? What happens to those who live, work and play in the city? Can the community members have a say in the development of the built environment in which they live?

Certainly planners and urban designers attempt to involve the community in the process of planning cities, although the extent to which they are successful is open to question. The main barriers to the attainment of Utopia in the city may be the obvious ones: resource constraints which restrict the funding available to finance design and development; socio-political priorities which leave urban design issues as secondary, rather than primary, priorities; poor management of the urban design and development process, which may result in a lack of coordination between those involved and/or lack of clarity in their respective roles and the inter-relationship between these roles.

3.2.2 Conservation and heritage

The built environment is dynamic in a changing world: buildings, their design, their construction and their uses evolve in response to change. Is the conservation of heritage inimical to the development of the city of the future? What problems and constraints are imposed upon the built-environment professions by society's wish to conserve the legacy of the past?

Traditionally, employment was often located within the same building as living space, or the two functions were sited in adjacent space. For example, shops or traditional workshops with living space built above have featured in societies from Europe to Asia. Today, the provision of offices or living spaces above retail space helps to retain mixed use and promotes activity and therefore a sense of community in an area. However, this co-location of working and living space is far less commonplace today than in traditional societies.

To the real estate developer, conservation can act as a constraint where planning and government policies and regulations prevent profitable redevelopment and development of sites within urban boundaries where there is demand for property. This constraint, however, sometimes turns into a profitable opportunity where traditional heritage is valued by purchasers, resulting in a premium value for property of a traditional/historic style.

The choice between conservation and new development is often a difficult one at central sites in any major city. The price of land in city centre locations is at a premium, whether the city is New York, London or Singapore, so that difficult choices have to be made as to its future use. Site redevelopment in order to provide contemporary multi-storey office accommodation will yield a higher rental value than would the conservation and refurbishment of an existing historic building on the site. One example of this conflict has arisen over the retaining some examples of traditional shop houses on prime sites in Singapore city rather than their demolition to make way for new buildings.

One benefit of retaining traditional architecture is that it can provide a centre for the retention of local character and culture within the context of increasingly global urban architecture. In this way, conservation areas can offer sites for relaxation and leisure for the local population and hence help to retain the identity of the individual city, ensuring that New York, London and Singapore can all retain a distinctive flavour.

Conservation is concerned with retaining elements of the past so that future generations can appreciate their heritage. The property stock available to be conserved is, however, of itself variable. For instance, today, the pressure is to modernise the interior of commercial property in order to make it compatible with the installation and maintenance requirements of computing and information technology, while retaining older exteriors. In the eighteenth and nineteenth centuries, the reverse was true: older interiors would be retained while a modern exterior was constructed on the front of the building. In many climates, the supply of heritage buildings is constrained because wooden structures have not survived. It is also notable that architectural and historic interest in the dwellings and workplaces of most of the populace, as distinct from the rich minority, has for the most part only emerged in the past fifty years. It is even more recently that heritage agencies in countries such as the UK have sought to retain selected sites and buildings from fifty years ago for conservation. Attitudes to the nature and quantity of desirable conservation have shifted over time and will doubtless continue to evolve as society's values and preferences change.

3.2.3 Leisure and the 24-hour city

The richer of the world's economies today share a common problem in relation to their urban development: real estate prices tend to be lower on the fringes than in the centre of the cities and so activity and people alike become priced out of the city centre. In this scenario, how can the city centre be reinvigorated?

One approach to solving this problem has been by tapping into another common feature of these richer economies. As household incomes rise, people can spend less time working in order to satisfy their basic needs for food and shelter – and so they have more non-work time in their lives to use as they wish. This increase in discretionary time is reflected in an expansion in time devoted to leisure activities and therefore expansion of the leisure industries that supply these needs.

If leisure can be located in the city centre, then people will visit the city in their leisure time. The centre will be kept alive – and will be lively – if leisure activities are taking place around the clock. Hence, the notion of the 24-hour city in which there is activity all day and all night long. This 24-hour activity brings with it a number of advantages. There are always people on the streets and so individuals feel more secure and safe. However, there are associated costs, such as maintaining cleanliness and staffing over such an extended period.

A successful leisure-based city centre, where people come to go to museums, to dine out, and to shop, requires active city centre management. It also requires a transparent statement of the costs and benefits associated with such a pattern of city centre life, and an understanding of how the costs should be apportioned between private suppliers and their customers on the one hand, and the public purse on the other. These questions also apply to the major issues of where people should live and work, and how they should travel. It is to these questions that we turn next.

3.2.4 Housing

Housing represents the single most important use of the land in urban areas so it is worth considering briefly some of the questions raised by those interested in housing:

- Where should houses be built?
- What housing densities are sustainable in today's city?
- What design requirements should be imposed in the interests of sustainability?
- What should be done if cost makes the price of housing too expensive for the most vulnerable members of society?

Where should houses be built?

The answer to the question of where houses should be built can be complex. In many countries, both those such as the UK and Japan, with high population densities, but also those with sizeable urban populations, there is a preference for re-using existing sites for residential development rather than allocating virgin land to housing. In terms of sustainability, such redevelopment of previously used sites has much to commend it.

It means that existing infrastructure, from drainage to roads, can be reused; communities can continue to develop; and land not previously built upon can be better safeguarded from urban sprawl. However, there are problems with attaining sustainable development through developing housing on brownfield sites. For example, the need to upgrade existing infrastructure will add to costs; where land is contaminated as a result of past use, there will be the costs of cleaning the site to an appropriate standard for residential development; where demolition of obsolete building is required, that will be an additional cost. In addition, there is commonly a difficulty in rebuilding confidence in an area that has become run down and semi-derelict. A poor reputation and lack of confidence do not contribute to successful redevelopment and rising property values. In such a scenario, the role of the public sector and public investment may be an essential ingredient in the process of rebuilding and regeneration.

The principle of mixed-use development, (siting residential development near to people's employment) is attractive. However, in practice attaining this objective is complicated by the increasing scale and complexity of employment and occupational patterns in contemporary society. The self-sufficient village community and the town dominated by a single employer are both increasingly models from the past. Schools and hospitals become larger and serve larger geographical areas; there is also increased specialisation and an expansion of producer services such as finance and marketing. Both these trends mean that, while sensitive and effective planning of mixed-use development can make some travel to and from work avoidable, some travel is unavoidably associated with the diversity of occupation and employment in modern societies. One interesting counter to this trend is the ability of information technology to enable more working from home, and this, in principle, may reduce the frequency of journeys to work although it is unlikely to eliminate them.

Design requirements and density

A major challenge for built-environment professionals is to help to provide sustainable housing through the use of environmentally friendly materials, as discussed in section 3.1.1, and through the appropriate use of energy and insulation, such as double and triple glazing. Such energy-efficient housing will incur lower running costs and therefore be more affordable to those who live there, in addition to being more sustainable. In the section on transport (section 3.2.5), the possibilities of minimising the impact of the private car upon residential development are discussed. Here, it can be noted that sustainable design for housing development should put people first, creating an environment that is safe and secure for pedestrians, including children.

The design concept of the compact city requires relatively high-density housing in order to increase accessibility and to reduce the need to travel. Higher density brings residents the benefits of proximity to services and facilities, in contrast to much of the extensive low-density suburban development of the last century. Development of three- and four-storey dwellings can appear spacious once there is adequate provision of communal space in the overall design.

Social housing provision

Whether in shanty towns or in run-down permanent housing, areas of social exclusion provide a challenge in most contemporary cities. Social exclusion is often associated with a vicious circle of poverty and decline in the environment, including housing. Where people are too poor to afford to pay for shelter, there is an important role for the public sector in housing provision. In many countries, a high proportion of the overall housing stock is built and managed by the public sector – in contrast, the proportion in the UK is now relatively small. So, there is often a major role for the public sector in housing provision and this is reflected in the provision of housing construction and management services by the public authorities.

One difficulty with the provision of social housing is matching supply to demand in the absence of market prices. Where people want and can afford to live will be influenced by employment opportunities, among other considerations. Provision of social housing in inner-city areas when employment opportunities are some distance away and transport costs are expensive may contribute to a cycle of unemployment and poverty rather than helping people to find employment and become more self-sufficient. It is not only the quantity of housing provision that is relevant, but also the size and quality of the dwellings provided. There will be little demand for three- and four-bedroom units in a society with small households, and little demand for one-bedroom units in a society where large families are more common. Some of the problems of achieving a match between housing demand and housing provision are common to both public and private-sector provision and are outlined below.

Private housing provision

In the UK, the majority of houses are provided through the private-sector. However, the private-sector housing market does not always operate smoothly, as is illustrated by the extensive discrepancies between supply and demand that were present in 2001. We shall use this example to illustrate some of the difficulties in answering the question of where houses should be built, and to demonstrate the implications of the housing market for the wider economy and society.

In the UK, the number of new houses built during 2001 in the private sector was the lowest for sixty years. In the same year, interest rates were historically as low as at any time during the past fifty years so that buyers could afford to borrow money in order to fund house purchase relatively cheaply. Consumer demand in the UK economy was, in general, buoyant. So what would be the likely effect upon house prices?

A prediction that house prices would have increased in the UK during 2001 would be correct: the rate of increase was typically over 10% in a year when inflation was below 3%.

The historically low rate of house building at a time of high demand suggests a shortage of supply. This would indicate that more houses should be built. The UK government estimates that an extra 152,000 homes a year should be built, against the 140,000 achieved in 2001. However, a specialist report indicates that a much higher figure of 225,000 may be needed in order to accommodate a population that is living longer and dwelling in smaller household units (Joseph Rowntree Foundation, 2002).

The UK planning process is criticised from some quarters for causing a restriction to the supply of new houses, both through limiting the availability of land for housing and so raising its price, and also through physically slowing down the processing of planning applications so that the rate of construction is constricted.

But the housing supply is more complex than this. An increase in quantity alone may not be enough to correct the type of imbalance in the private housing market outlined above.

In practice, more people are living alone in the UK than was previously the case. As a result, there is more demand for smaller dwelling units. Rising living standards and expectations mean that demand is for better-quality housing, leaving some poor-quality property residualised. And, as ever with the built environment, location matters. Demand is not evenly spatially distributed: excess demand is particularly acute in growth regions of the UK, notably the south-east of England, and in some rural locations. Whether further housing should be built in these preferred locations is controversial: a challenge for the contemporary built environment.

If more houses are not built in the expanding economy of south-east England, then house prices will continue to rise in the region and labour shortages will recur. Does it matter if house prices increase? In the south-east of England nearly 75% of householders own their own property, so a 10% increase in house prices will benefit this affluent 75%. There are associated issues of income distribution – 'equity', in the jargon of economics. The poorer 25% become further disadvantaged as the gap between rich and poor is widened. The cumulative effect of percentage changes makes this result even more stark. The owner of a £100,000 house gains £10,000 through a 10% increase in property values, while the owner of a £400,000 house gains £40,000 through a 10% increase in property values. The spatial income distribution across the economy becomes more uneven too – and this, in an economy where over 90% of higher-rate income tax revenue was derived from the south-east of England during the 1990s (Temple, 1994).

One major aspect of the challenge presented by the current state of the UK housing market is therefore whether or not to encourage or even to allow further house building in the south-east region of England. The advantage of building in this growing region is that the demand is there and a matched supply should help to take the pressure out of house prices. But would further housing development in the south-east and its cities be sustainable?

Housing represents a major land and building use in the built environment and, socially, provision of shelter through housing is a recognised human need. This section has therefore introduced some of the key questions in relation to housing provision and illustrated some of the ways in which housing relates to the core built-environment subjects.

3.2.5 Transport

One characteristic of the Utopian city is a minimum transport requirement, in so far as people's work and leisure is co-located in a densely populated urban core. This reduces the need for daily travel and so reduces travel time, energy consumption and the environmental damage associated with transport.

Transport provision raises a variety of issues: it requires the allocation of land to that specific use; it can generate pollutants; it may be provided through the public or the private sector, or through partnership between them. Transport may be powered by renewable or by non-renewable energy sources. The provision of good, frequent, inexpensive bus/tram/train services can reduce car use, as can adequate provision for cyclists and pedestrians.

Pollution caused by transport damages buildings in cities – but, more importantly, it damages the quality of the air and therefore the health of the city community, in particular the young, old and deprived. Provision of effective and affordable public transport, using non-pollutant energy sources, and the encouragement of walking and cycling, are therefore even more important for a city to be sustainable.

Until recently, many urban design policies have been driven by the need to accommodate road transport, not least within residential development. The idea that urban design is accomplished through the provision of a road network, followed by the design of housing, has been challenged since the turn of the century as being inimical to the attainment of sustainable urban design. A more sustainable urban design will designate housing first, in residential spaces, and residualise the road network and parking provision to comply with the needs of residential provision rather than the other way round. The compact city will have higher-density housing, less reliance on private vehicles as a mode of transport, and enhanced public transport provision and public spaces (see, for example, Rogers and Power, 2000).

For a country such as the UK, the drive for more sustainability in urban design poses some real dilemmas. The price of private cars has reduced in recent years and it is expected that there will be more cars on the roads in five years' time than there are at present. On the other hand, the government is moving away from the need for a minimum car-parking provision in new residential developments towards a maximum allowable provision of 1.5 parking spaces for each private dwelling, in the interests of discouraging private cars as a mode of transport.

However, recent research (Stubbs, 2002) has found that private residents do not necessarily share the government's and urban designer's taste for sustainability. Residents wish to have private dedicated car parking in the interests of convenience and also as part of their investment in the future market value of their property. The residential developers who build housing are unlikely to ignore the views of their customers and so there is little incentive for developers to provide wholly car-free residential developments.

In North America, urban development during the second half of the twentieth century was notably extensive, with considerable separation between housing and employment leading to long-distance commuting in private cars for those able to afford it. The urban ring has been expanding, with the provision of additional road capacity at the existing edge of urban areas leading to further increases in commuting distances, not only to work but also for access to schools, shops and leisure facilities. The result has been increasing transport and environmental problems in many American cities. For those unable to afford commuting to work by car, there has been a circumscription of employment opportunities, causing social problems for those on low incomes in urban areas. Low-density development and urban sprawl have also resulted in further environmental degradation, so exacerbating environmental problems.

In North America, the 'compact city' approach has its parallel in the movement for smart growth, aimed at producing reinvestment in existing urban areas (rather than their further expansion); mixed use, to bring housing and employment closer together; pedestrian-friendly development; and development based around public transport hubs in order to persuade people to become less reliant upon private transport. Such smart growth requires positive action by city authorities, taking a holistic approach to issues of the environment, transport, housing and economic development. It also requires positive incentives to regenerate older urban areas so that they can be re-enlivened; and transit-oriented development to encourage people away from reliance upon the private car.

So, is it possible to attain a workable solution that recognises the importance of the private car to households whose members form urban society whilst attaining an urban design centred upon such sustainable concepts as the compact city and greatly reduced space allocated to parking provision? Stubbs found that 'security and proximity to home were identified as the most important design considerations in parking layouts' (Stubbs, 2002, p. 234). Development density could be increased, and these priorities acknowledged, by removing built garages and using rear courtyards and on street parking in new urban developments. In parallel, public transport needs to be improved in order to persuade people that there is a real alternative to private transport in the sustainable city of the twenty-first century.

Transport systems typically face problems analogous to those associated with the built environment in general: transport assets are long lasting and expensive. As a result, like property, it is neither easy nor inexpensive to alter transport provision as the built environment evolves. Roads and railways alike become redundant as the pattern of settlement and economic activity evolves. Different societies and governments have a tradition of spending different proportions of GDP upon their transport infrastructure. For example, the British government spent less than a quarter of the sum spent by the Swiss government per head of population during 2000. This may provide one simple explanation of the fact that the Swiss economy benefits from a more sophisticated integrated public transport system than does the British economy.

A major difficulty faced by many contemporary societies emanates from consumer preferences as expressed through the marketplace: as individuals become richer they express a clear preference for owning and using private cars rather than public transport. This preference provides the challenge for transport planners today: public transport modes are more environmentally friendly, and in areas of high population density, often more efficient than the private car. But people have to be encouraged, persuaded or forced into not using cars as their preferred means of transport.

The challenge for an effective transport system is to be rapid; to satisfy customer needs; and also to minimise environmental damage. The debate centred around these transport issues can be summarised as: Can or should society seek to restrict people's travel or should society encourage the provision of cheap and environmentally friendly transport as a priority?

One policy that has been applied in order to tackle the problem of city centre congestion and pollution caused by cars is that of restricting the use of the private car by charging for car use. For example, in Singapore for several years there has been a charge payable for all cars entering the city centre during peak hours. The aim is to reduce the levels of congestion and pollution in the city. The policy is practical because there was already effective public transport provision through the metro system and both the city centre and its commuter suburbs are geographically compact. Parking is provided adjacent to the metro stations so that commuters can drive to their neighbourhood metro rather than driving into the city centre.

There are benefits for those who continue to drive into the city centre under schemes such as this: if the roads are emptier than before, then their journey times will be quicker. But there is a distributional issue here: is it fair that those who can afford to pay for the privilege can benefit relative to others who are less well off?

The introduction of road pricing in central London has also been an acknowledged success, reducing road congestion and increasing use of public transport. Like Singapore, London has a high population density and an extensive public transport system that was well used prior to the introduction of road charging.

In spite of these positive examples, it is not yet entirely clear how successful road charging in city centres would be as a more general policy. There may be costs in terms of business lost within an extensive conurbation where one city imposes charges while another competing city close by does not do likewise. For example, in the north-west of England, if Manchester introduced charging while Liverpool did not, then some businesses might prefer to relocate to Liverpool rather than being based in Manchester.

This example again highlights the difficulty of attaining sustainability in practice, and also the importance of transport policy and provision as an element of that sustainability in our cities.

3.2.6 The sustainable city?
Cities, and in particular city centres, thrive on accessibility. If it is quick, easy and cheap to move around the city centre, and to move in and out of it, then the city is likely to thrive. Good accessibility becomes an important element determining the extent to which a particular city centre has a comparative

advantage over those of rival cities. A city centre will be a preferred location for economic activity if movement is cheap in terms of distance, time, and convenience of travel. Good accessibility requires good transport facilities, but also a thriving labour market and good provision of service facilities to support business organisations that locate in the city.

The benefits of accessibility will increase demand for location in the city. In turn, this increased demand for city centre locations will push up the price of property in the city centre. Where this happens, high-value, high-status activities remain in the city centre while lower-value, lower-status activities are pushed out towards the edge of the city. The high status of expensive city centre locations explains why city centre addresses are often the preferred location for the head offices of large organisations. These offices are seeking to maximise the benefits that they can gain from the perceived external economies of scale associated with a city centre location. These benefits include ready access to market information, both explicit and tacit, and to service providers.

Cities are dynamic. Migrants from rural to urban areas are attracted to the city in order to try to secure better paid employment: a pattern readily observed in many countries of the world today. Immigrants arriving in a different country normally cluster in its major cities. In both cases, the effect is to contribute to a pool of labour in the city, adding to its attractiveness to employers. At the same time, immigrants add to the cultural diversity and richness of urban life, adding to its attractiveness to employees.

However, commercial and residential rent levels remain a major problem of urban development: the differential in commercial rents between the city centre and the suburb can easily be threefold, and often much higher. A successful city tends to push out lower-value activities towards its periphery because of the high costs of city centre location. Similarly, the workforce is pushed away from the expensive centre. This increases the distance between jobs and the housing for those supplying the labour to undertake those jobs – not necessarily a sustainable path.

The very accessibility that triggers the success of a city centre can therefore sow the seeds of future problems. Accessibility results in high rents; easy transport access results in congestion and environmental pollution. The benefits of the city centre can all too easily transform into the costs of a city centre location. Where these costs are specific to a single city centre, then that city may lose its comparative advantage in relation to competing centres. Economic development will shift away from the congested city towards a less expensive and less congested location.

Where these costs are common to many cities, there may be a trend towards counter-urbanisation. Counter-urbanisation sees economic activity moving away from city centres more generally. Some commentators have remarked upon a doughnut effect that leaves city centres as undesirable locations, unattractive to economic activity – and therefore unsustainable.

In mature economies such as the USA and UK, speculative commercial property developers find it cheaper and more attractive to build new property on new greenfield sites rather than to develop property on brownfield land in city centres that may be subject to contamination from its previous use. Again, such an outward spreading of commercial development is not contributing to a sustainable built environment.

Speculative commercial property developers make money by anticipating the future property requirements of potential real estate investors and occupiers. When their expectations are accurate, they are profitable. When their expectations prove to be inaccurate, they lose money. At present, there is little to indicate that commercial users of real estate are swayed by considerations of sustainability in choosing their location. As a result, if the property market is left solely to commercial pressures there is little evidence to suggest that real estate development will enhance urban sustainability.

It is in this context that the influence of the planning framework can be significant. Planning systems and procedures can offer incentives to the developers in order to encourage them to offer mixed-use development, to erect energy-efficient buildings, and to redevelop brownfield sites.

Overall, it is difficult to identify the extent to which recent urban development has become more sustainable, as we lack reliable indicators through which to measure it. The drive for sustainability continues to be impeded by the perceived tensions between enhanced environmental sustainability and enhanced economic growth – although a growing body of academic opinion is suggesting that, in the long term, these goals are complementary rather than incompatible. In the short term, there continue to be conflicts between sustainability and economic expansion: for example, it is increasingly recognised that significant improvements to public transport provision are a necessary precursor to restricting the use of cars, but public authorities are often reluctant to make the necessary financial commitment.

The nature of the interdependence of the constituents of the urban built environment means that all the built-environment professions need to work together and towards greater sustainability if it is to become an attainable goal for our cities. As the above paragraphs have shown, planning, urban design and real estate are all directly involved in this process – as are the architects, builders and engineers! In 2002, a Royal Institution of Chartered Surveyors (RICS) Report opined that the property industry had not yet really grasped the importance of urban sustainability (RICS Foundation, 2002). Attaining urban sustainability is undoubtedly a contemporary challenge on a global scale: one that is particularly acute in the huge, rapidly expanding cities of the developing world.

Can today's city attain sustainability in the sense of meeting today's needs without compromising the needs of future generations? It is questionable whether or not it can: what is clear, however, is that the attempt requires the cooperation of all built-environment professionals.

▶ 3.3 Developing the built environment

The final section of this chapter looks at the development of the built environment, including a brief consideration of three different examples of this development. The first example looks at urban regeneration based upon waterside redevelopment, while the second considers a recent urban site redevelopment scheme in London. In contrast, the third and final example looks at a rural development. One theme running through this section of the chapter illustrates the ways in which the different Built Environment subject professionals work together, while also providing some examples of their distinctive roles within the development of the built environment. In this way, this final section of the chapter acts as a link between Part One of this book, which has outlined some of the themes and challenges facing the built environment, and Part Two, which focuses upon individual subjects.

3.3.1 Financing development of the built environment

Typically, buildings are relatively expensive to construct and to own – their construction and ownership is accordingly financed through borrowing rather than through the medium of cash payment. Buildings are also relatively long lasting – and may prove difficult to sell on to a new purchaser. For these reasons, buildings are comparatively illiquid as an asset. This means that lending money against the security of a building, or investing in buildings, can be relatively risky compared with other available categories of asset. Therefore, property investment and finance is an important aspect of the built environment whether commercial or residential property.

Government can affect the amount and type of property finance available at a particular time by altering the tax treatment of such finance and therefore influencing its attractiveness relative to other financial investments.

The UK is unusual in having a highly developed market geared towards the provision of finance to enable individuals to purchase residential property for their own use – that is, for owner occupation. In many countries, residential property is more commonly rented and so finance is primarily designed in order to enable the purchase of property for rental to others. While, in either case, lenders will be anxious to minimise the likelihood of a borrower defaulting on a loan, this element of risk becomes higher when lending is to the wider population rather than primarily to landlords. For this reason, borrowing in order to finance private ownership of residential property is subject to relatively rigorous risk assessment on the part of lenders.

The calculations underpinning possible borrowing in order to finance the private ownership of residential property are relatively straightforward. For example, an individual wishes to purchase a property costing £100,000 today. Once the lending bank believes the borrower creditworthy, the person will be able to borrow a proportion of the £100,000 over, say, a ten- or twenty-year period at a rate of interest slightly above the current average interest rate. (The surcharge on the interest rate will be small because the value of the property will act as security for the loan, making it a relatively low-risk transaction for the lender.) The borrower will then finance the repayment of the loan from the current flow of income over the period of the loan.

The financing of commercial property, and of residential property that is to be rented out to tenants, operates upon slightly different principles. This is because the borrower expects to repay the loan from the stream of income received from the future tenants of the property.

For example, let us look at the instance where an individual wishes to purchase a residential property costing £100,000 today in order to let it out to tenants. The money borrowed in order to finance the purchase will be paid back from the revenue stream of rental income received from the tenants of the property. So, for example, if the anticipated interest charges on a loan of £100,000 are £5,000, and the anticipated rental income is £125,000, then the person may anticipate a profit of £20,000. Should the property require expenditure of £20,000 to refurbish it prior to letting, there will be no profit. In addition, the very simple calculation outlined here makes no allowance for the effects of the timescale over which the rental income will accrue. Normally we assume that money available now has a higher value than money that may become available in the future.

Sometimes commercial and residential properties are built or refurbished by the intended user of that property. On other occasions, property developers take the initiative and develop buildings on sites with a view to selling or letting the buildings to future users. In this case, the developer acts as an intermediary and also absorbs some of the risk associated with the development of the buildings. The basic underlying principles are the same as those outlined above – only the numbers are usually larger!

For example, a developer acquires a site for £1,000,000 with a view to building commercial office space on the site. In addition to the construction costs of the offices, say £2,500,000, the developer needs to allow for other important categories of expenditure: the payment of fees to other professionals such as lawyers, architects and surveyors, say £150,000; and marketing costs, say £100,000. This leaves the developer with costs of £2,750,000 in addition to the original payment of £1,000,000 for the site – that is, a total cost of £3,750,000. If the expected rental value of the offices is £400,000 each year, will the development be profitable for the developer?

It depends. For instance, it depends upon:

- the cost of borrowing finance in order to fund the proposed development;
- the timescale over which the borrowing and the rental income are to be calculated – and the likelihood of changes in the rate of price inflation during that time;
- the anticipated illiquidity of the investment and therefore the extent of the risk associated with the project.
- the alternative return (or yield) that the developer could have earned by investing the original million-pound outlay in another type of investment – economists refer to this as the 'opportunity cost' of the chosen investment.

So matters of property finance easily become complex (issues concerned with risk and timescale are investigated in texts about property investment such as Baum and Crosby, 1995). If you are a student who finds this complexity to be challenging and interesting, then you may wish to study this area in greater depth to gain more specialist knowledge. If not, then remember that a basic understanding of the principles of finance will prove useful during any professional career in the built environment.

3.3.2 Private and public sector: Who invests?

The ability to move financial capital relatively freely around much of the world has resulted in the globalisation of capital and capital markets. Accordingly, in some parts of the property market the market is effectively international, and there is global mobility of ownership between the American continent, Europe, the Middle East, the Far East and Australasia.

One disadvantage of private-sector investment and development in the built environment is that it can be driven by a relatively short-term view, whilst large-scale property development is a long-term activity. Investment activity in property tends to increase as the economic cycle reaches towards its peak – and then finance may be withdrawn as the cycle moves back into recession. This was the experience of both Japan and the UK at the beginning of the 1990s. Public-sector investment in property may, in principle, be less dependent upon such short-term considerations but – in practice – it also often varies over time in response to the current and expected public funding and taxation situation.

The development of the built environment can be undertaken either by the public sector or by private developers, the balance between private and public activity varying between different countries and also varying over time. The benefits of private developers are that they will proactively seek out opportunities, be prepared to take risks and, in general, adopt an entrepreneurial approach to development, whether of residential or commercial property. Public-sector development is more risk-averse and more likely to be motivated by social, as well as narrowly economic, needs. The public sector is accordingly more likely to provide social housing for those households who cannot otherwise afford decent housing provision, and to provide public space and social amenities.

The way in which the built environment is developed and financed and the nature of that development is therefore affected by the relative roles of the private sector and public sector. The private sector is primarily driven by the profit motive while the public sector is more accountable to wider social needs. (The attempt to capture the benefits of an effective private sector and to deal with resulting social distortions through the economic analysis of the relative private and social costs and benefits was introduced earlier in this chapter.)

There is therefore a case to be made for the intervention of the public sector in some aspects of the built environment, such as the provision of public spaces and social amenities in cities. However, there is debate as to how extensive should be the intervention and to what extent a government, either local, regional or national, should attempt to change the direction of underlying private-sector market trends. The argument against public subsidy in relation to the property market can be illustrated by the viewpoint expressed by Macintosh and Sykes that

> as a general principle, an institution or property developer should not purchase industrial property in any location which is entitled to any from of government grant or assistance. The very fact that a particular location merits some form of financial assistance from public funds indicates that there is little if any demand for industrial property in that area. (Macintosh and Sykes, 1985, p. 158)

In recent decades, there has been much exploration of the notion of private-sector/public-sector partnerships designed to harness the benefits of the private sector and those of the public sector in relation to the development of the built environment. While the relevant issues are explored in detail elsewhere (see, for example, Temple, 1994, pp. 208–15), a summary will be illuminating here.

Essentially, the argument for public-sector/private-sector partnership hinges upon the nature of the benefits to be derived from developments such as major urban regeneration projects. There are benefits to society, including less dereliction and an improved visual environment; but there are also benefits to individuals, such as the increased rental and sale value of the buildings located in the regenerated area. It can therefore be argued that both the private sector and the public sector gain the benefits from urban regeneration and therefore that both should contribute to the cost.

In relation to raising finance, the public sector is seen as a lower risk than the private sector – this is because the public sector does not (normally) go bankrupt whereas private companies can end up bankrupt and unable to repay their debts. On the other hand, competitive pressures and the presence of the profit motive can make the private sector more efficient, and therefore less costly, than the public sector. So, a partnership between the two sectors can yield access to finance at lower cost, and implementation of the development project at lower cost – as long as competitive pressures and cost cutting are not detrimental to quality.

3.3.3 Regeneration: Waterside development

The historic importance of water as a transport route and the international use of boats as a mode of transport have resulted in the development of settlements, including some large cities, adjacent to water. The historic and economic importance of such regions and so of these cities has ebbed and flowed as, in some cases, has the water. Consequently, semi-derelict areas of towns and cities fronting onto water have become an international phenomenon from Asia to Europe to the Americas.

The redevelopment and regeneration of these waterside areas has therefore been a challenge facing a wide variety of local and central governments, in a wide variety of economies and climates. There are examples of redeveloped waterside areas from Singapore to the Netherlands, from Canada to Ecuador. So, what are the common characteristics of these areas and what are the features of the more successful regeneration projects?

Prior to regeneration, there is decline and dereliction that bring with them a lack of economic activity, lack of pedestrian flow, poverty, crime, social deprivation, and a poor quality of spatial environment. How can such areas be improved?

In the UK, the Commission for Architecture and the Built Environment (2001) challenged many previously held ideas on the cost of quality urban design. Their work set out to quantify what was meant by 'quality' in urban design and to appraise the financial consequences of pursuing such provision in new development projects. After studying a series of case studies the researchers concluded that:

> Good urban design does add economic value . . . [and that] high quality urban design is attractive to key sections of the rental, investment and owner/occupier market, who are prepared to pay extra for better quality design.

By way of example, one of their case studies dealt with Barbirolli Square in central Manchester. This involved a 1-hectare redevelopment of former railway land to create a cultural and office district consisting of a concert hall, two office blocks and a café/bar. A public space was created, linking and opening up a former canal basin. The site was considered by the researchers to be reasonably well connected, and created 'a new landmark gateway to Manchester'. Subsequently, the offices have commanded high rents and an economic ripple effect is evident in the surrounding area.

Where regeneration is successful, it can be a powerful force for change that brings back prosperity to the locality. Some successful projects focus upon provision for leisure and tourism, offering shops, restaurants, open spaces for public events, museums, walkways and waterways. Larger-scale projects, such as the regeneration of the London Docklands riverside along the Thames, have involved leisure and residential development but also significant new commercial and office development.

This major London redevelopment has been criticised on a number of occasions for lack of social responsibility: for failing to provide adequate social housing for former residents and for failing to provide adequate local employment for the same group. The extent to which redevelopment follows a social agenda varies, being largely, although not wholly, dependent upon who is the provider of redevelopment finance.

A public, socially oriented agenda is more likely to predominate where funding is from the public sector. A profit-oriented agenda is more likely where funding is from the private sector. In a number of countries, attempts have been made to bring together the best of both worlds through the formation of public–private partnerships (PPPs).

Where redevelopment is to be ethically and environmentally aware, there is a clear role both for planners, in relation to physical planning but also environmental impact assessment, and for historic and natural conservationists. These professionals emphasise the importance of social value so as to balance the interests of those built-environment professionals whose prime aim is to maximise economic value from development.

Successful redevelopment in the public interest requires cooperation and partnership among commercial real estate interests, financial providers, environmental groups and local government. Urban designers play a lead role in the development and project management of regeneration, bringing together architects, planners and the other main interested parties. In many cases, however, there remains a tension between urban designers and town planners on the one hand, and real estate developers on the other hand. The reasons for, and the effects of, this tension are explained more fully in the following example.

3.3.4 St Paul's Cathedral, London

This example illustrates some of the connections between architectural design, urban design, town planning, real estate development and real estate valuation.

Paternoster Square, an area of over 88,000 square metres next to the land-mark of St Paul's Cathedral in London, is being redeveloped. The cost of the redevelopment is estimated at around £200 million, yielding an end invest-ment value of over £400 million. It is rare for such a large-scale redevelop-ment opportunity to arise on a sensitive site in central London. The development has been controversial and subject to delay – the final scheme went forward after a ten-year delay, five different owners, and at least three different plans. As with all new developments and redevelopments, building up the confidence of real estate investors and occupiers has been crucial. When a well-known bank agreed to lease a significant amount of space in the vicinity in 1998, it provided a major boost to the attraction of other occupiers to the proposed redevelopment.

For the real estate developer, the optimal outcome of the development or redevelopment process is either the maximum increase in the investment asset value of the property or the maximisation of the rental income stream to be obtained from it.

The optimal outcome of the development or redevelopment process for society is the maximum increase in the social value of the property, one aspect of which is its future sustainability. The role of the planner is to act on behalf of society as the guardian of the social interest.

If we consider the difference between the objective of the developer and that of the planner, we can see that there may well be conflict between their different interests in the development process: there is certainly an inherent tension.

The possible outcomes of the development process on this central urban site, or a similar one, are now considered in more detail. Some possible outcomes are outlined as follows:

- The site was predominantly used by commercial office space, and so an increase in the mix of uses on the site would contribute to its sustain-ability from the planners' viewpoint. For example, redevelopment could result in a change from solely office buildings to a wider mix, including retail and leisure sites. The latter would be attractive both to tourists and to those working locally. In practice, the redevelopment is likely to be 90% office space compared with around 10% retail.

- In this specific example, there could be a reduction in the density of build-ing on the site. This would enable an opening up of the view of St Paul's

Cathedral, which would also increase the natural sunlight reaching the site. Both these factors would benefit the tourists visiting the locality and also those people working there. In general, urban design aims to utilise redevelopment opportunities in order to enhance the provision of urban vistas and the quality of public spaces, so improving the overall experience of the urban environment.

• Architecturally, redevelopment offers an opportunity to improve the design and aesthetics of buildings and groups of buildings on the site. In this case, such an improvement could be brought about by the replacement of existing 1960s concrete buildings, most of which were built in the same style. One objective of the actual redevelopment is to commission several different architects so as to obtain a greater diversity of architectural styles on the site.

• A contrasting outcome from the redevelopment could be greater obstruction of the existing view of St Paul's Cathedral. This would arise from the development of high-density, high-rise office buildings on the site in order to maximise its rental and asset value. Supporters of further skyscraper development in central London argue in favour of higher-density office space in order to expand the supply of commercial offices so as to attract more investment and employment into the city. Their argument is that, without this provision, businesses seeking large-scale office buildings will move to less central locations.

Earlier in this chapter, the tension between the conservation of traditional buildings and the maximisation of commercial real estate development was highlighted. This tension can now be extended to the more general question of how far opportunities for the redevelopment of expensive central city sites should be used in order to provide improved urban design and public spaces, or to enable the private sector to generate more revenue – which will, in turn, provide more taxation revenue to the local government to fund its services. So, further to the earlier discussion in section 3.1.3 of this chapter: what price the view of St Paul's?

3.3.5 A slate quarry in the English Lake District

In contrast to the above example, which focused upon a sensitive urban site in the centre of a capital city, this second case study considers a proposal to extend an existing slate quarry in the English Lake District. In particular, we look at this example in relation to the different subject disciplines you may study under the umbrella of the Built Environment.

The English Lake District is a small area in the north-west of England characterised, as its name implies, by scenic features of lakes and hills. The beauty of the landscape is such that the Lake District has been classified as an area of natural beauty of international importance, in addition to being a designated National Park.

With the exceptions of tourism and agriculture, there is little employment available within the rural heart of the Lake District. One exception is the employment offered by the few remaining quarries extracting natural slate. Slate provides an important local material for building, and in particular roofing, in the local vernacular architectural style.

Recently the local slate quarries have experienced increasing demand, not only from local sources, but also from further afield because natural slate has become a fashionable material for interior uses in buildings such as domestic kitchen flooring. A local slate quarry therefore wishes to expand its operations and to construct an additional small office building from which to manage its enhanced scale of operations. Table 3.1 indicates the broad range of issues raised by a proposal of this nature and how they relate to the different subject perspectives from which we study the built environment.

Table 3.1 Issues and subjects

Issue raised	*Relevant subject*
Can the visual impact of the enlarged quarry and its activities be minimised?	Architecture, landscape architecture, and design
Can the environmental impact of the proposed new building be minimised?	Architecture, building
Is the enlarged quarry going to produce more pollution, for example through the release of underground gases, and can this be reduced to an acceptable level?	Building, environmental management
Are existing buildings on the site, and nearby, structurally safe if the quarry expansion goes ahead?	Building surveying
What effect will the construction work have on local roads and communities and how can this be contained?	Construction management
How can we balance the need to provide employment in rural communities with the need to conserve the natural environment?	Planning
What effect will the extended quarry have upon the value of the surrounding agricultural land and nearby dwellings?	Real estate management

Part Two
Subjects and Courses

4 Curriculum and content

This chapter introduces the curriculum and content of Built Environment courses at university, in order to illustrate both some of their common elements, but also some of their diversity. The principal subject disciplines covered in the chapter are Architecture, Building and Construction Management, Planning, Real Estate and Surveying.

The diversity of specialist approachs to, and interpretation of, the main subject disciplines at different higher education institutions means that there is a limit to the standardisation of the curriculum across different courses with similar titles: however, the professional bodies ensure an element of commonality for those courses with professional accreditation. In addition, in the UK the Quality Assurance Agency for Higher Education has supervised the writing of Subject Benchmark Statements that cover all undergraduate degree course provision. These Statements aim to ensure that there is a minimum standard for all degrees awarded, and that all students graduating with a similar degree will have a minimum set of similar skills and competencies.

What follows in this chapter is some generic guidance as to the nature of the curriculum and its content, reinforced, for many of the subjects covered, by a specialist commentary from an expert in the field.

The chapter is not intended as a substitute for detailed course-specific information from individual universities, nor for subject textbooks! Rather, it is designed to help students see the relationships between the bridging themes and challenges discussed in Chapters 2 and 3 and the individual subjects that they may be interested in studying.

▶ 4.1 Architecture

Architecture is centred upon the design of buildings, whether the creation of new buildings or making changes to the design of existing buildings. Architects may be concerned with a single building, with one part of that building, or with a linked group of buildings. While architecture centres upon the design process, the architect is also involved in the planning process that precedes the design, and in the construction process that sees the design develop from a set of drawings to the final building. The architect therefore needs to understand the role of other built-environment professionals involved in the planning, design and construction of buildings and the way in which their expertise relates to the expertise of these other professionals.

Buildings are three-dimensional objects and therefore it is vital that students are able to develop and to work with three-dimensional objects and spaces. Their designs must be aesthetically pleasing, while working as social spaces within which human interactions can take place effectively, and also draw upon current building techniques and technology. The skills of the architect and the study of architecture are therefore highly diverse and integrative, encompassing a wide range of skills and subject disciplines.

Architecture is focused around the creativity of design and so the design process conditions much of the pedagogic approach to learning and teaching in architecture. Learning, teaching and assessment are centred on design-project work conducted in the design studio. The design studio is a characteristic feature of architectural education and is the place where students create and display their work in progress and their finished design work. The ability to display work in progress and to discuss it with student peers and with staff in the studio means that formative feedback is vital to the successful progress of the student's design work. Architecture students have to be able to make and to listen to constructive critical comment, to internalise that commentary, reflect upon it and make positive use of it in order to take forward their own design work.

The Architecture curriculum also incorporates the study of the theory and history of architecture, so that students learn to understand the influences of the past upon today's buildings, cities and societies. These aspects of architecture are closely linked to study of the arts and humanities. In contrast, architecture students also learn about the technology of buildings and, in particular, how building technology interacts with the climate and the development of a sustainable environment. A few decades ago, buildings were designed to be insulated from the external environment, relying upon high levels of artificial energy use to provide lighting, heating and cooling. Today the emphasis is upon a more sustainable approach to building design that uses local climatic conditions and seeks to reduce energy use in the design and functioning of buildings.

In addition, the architect needs to understand the contractual and management relationships between the architect, the client, the builder and other key professionals involved in a construction project. For this reason, an element of contract law and management will normally form a part of the curriculum.

In addition to the core Architecture curriculum, there are courses that emphasise the technological aspects of architecture and the construction of buildings. These courses in Architectural Technology place less emphasis upon the humanities and more emphasis upon the engineering aspects of architecture. Courses such as Interior Design and Interior Architecture focus upon the inside design of a building, rather than its exterior appearance. In contrast, Landscape Architecture is primarily concerned with the relationship between a building, or group of buildings, and the environment within which it is placed.

4.1.1 Architecture

A specialist perspective from Helena Webster

Architecture is not the world's oldest profession but its antiquity is unassailable. The existence of architects is documented as far back as the third millennium before Christ although, according to Spiro Kostoff, there is graphic evidence of architectural practice in Asia Minor as far back as the seventh millennium BC. Hence, it may be reasonably claimed that architects came into existence at the time there was a societal demand for large or complex buildings, if only because someone had to conceive the building forms before construction could begin. Therefore the elemental role of the architect was from earliest times, and remains today, to conceive sound, robust and aesthetically meaningful buildings and to supply concrete representations of them so that others might construct them.

Although the formalisation of the practice of architecture into a profession in Britain did not occur until the late nineteenth century, evidence suggests that, throughout history, societal patterns have conscribed opportunities for architects and set the bar for their social standing. For instance, in ancient Egypt the building of monuments, such as the pyramids, had a significant social and economic impact and as a consequence the chief state architect belonged to the elite of the governing hierarchy. Likewise, in eighteenth-century Britain the practice of architecture, largely limited to the design of stately homes and palaces, was considered a suitable vocation for a civilised gentleman and the title was largely restricted to members of the aristocracy such as Lord Burlington and James Chambers.

More recently, in post-war Britain architects were considered as key players in the reconstruction of the war-torn cities and the provision of much needed social housing. Such was the centrality of the architects' social role in the post-war period that by the early 1970s some 55 per cent of the architecture profession worked for public bodies. However, by the latter part of the twentieth century, society noticed that the real legacy of the heroic period of post-war reconstruction was unloved and poorly constructed mass housing, and towns torn apart by vast and ugly road systems. The resulting public and government discontent with the architectural profession, most famously voiced by Prince Charles in a speech to the Royal Institute of British Architects on its 150th anniversary, in which he chastised architects for being self-serving and disconnected from the public opinion, coincided with a series of other events that together virtually decimated the profession.

At governmental level, the government gradually dismembered the public architects' departments, preferring to let design contracts out to private companies, many of which were non-architect led. Additionally, the government commissioned a series of reports into the construction industry, such as the Egan Report and the Latham Report, which found evidence of poor teamwork and poor-quality management across the industry as a whole, and criticised architects particularly for being ill-prepared, particularly in terms of team working, the size of practices (in 2000, 70% of the 5,000 architectural practices in Britain employed fewer than six people) and managerial skills, to respond to large building contracts and new methods of procuring buildings.

At a professional level, the architects' fixed fee scales were abolished and as a result competitive fee bidding reduced the financial viability of practice. At a public level, clients were no longer convinced that architects either added significant value to building projects or were good at leading the building team, and as a result started to use other members of the construction industry, such as project managers and surveyors, to procure buildings. Indeed, by the late 1980s the architect's role became so marginalised that they were often known as 'skin men', i.e. they only designed how the building looked from the outside.

However, after the low point in the 1980s, architecture and the profession began to find a new *raison d'être*. In the last 20 years there have been three major forces: the rapid development of digital technology, technological developments in the building sciences, and the rise of globalisation, that have altered the context for architectural practice, demanded architectural responses and as a consequence given architecture and architects a new life. Most significantly, during this period architects have been able to reassert their traditional position as professionals serving society, by framing their responses to these changes within a new ethical paradigm, the notion of sustainability. World summits in Rio and Tokyo successfully galvanised world leaders into the realisation that they must take immediate action to safeguard the world's resources for future generations. Hence, in recent years world governments have actively promoted social, economic and environmental initiatives with the aim of realising a more sustainable future.

In Britain, architects have been key players in the quest for sustainability. Currently architects are involved in developing and implementing government policy in the areas of urban and regional development (through Regional Development Agencies), specific urban design projects (through the Commission for Architecture and the Built Environment (CABE) and the Urban Task Force), housing improvement and new housing provision (through local government, European Union funding and the Housing Forum), research into the development of building types and technology (through the Movement for Innovation and the Building Research Establishment) and the design of new procurement methods and contracts (through the Construction Industry Council, the Lean Construction Institute and the Group for Lean Thinking).

A critical part of the sustainability debate has been an attempt to understand the relationship of the local to the global. Here again, architects have been making a vital contribution, particularly in relation to the issue of local and regional identity. Following the lead of Europe, where architecture and cities have traditionally been high on the political and cultural agenda, the British government has recently begun to invest in high-quality public projects, most notably the Millennium-funded projects such as the London Eye, and the Lottery-funded projects such as the Eden Project, that have succeeded in exciting the public and thereby reviving the belief that architecture can be culturally meaningful, challenging and progressive. Projects such as the Magna Science Adventure Centre in Rotherham have shown how local identity can be both reinforced and extended by architecture without retreating to historical stylistic pastiche. Slowly, the private sector is also realising that quality architecture can add real value to building projects, providing 'flag ship' imagery as well as enhancing 'fitness for purpose' and reducing long-term maintenance and energy costs. Additionally, businesses are also realising the value of using architects to help them to reflect generally on the efficacy of the spatial dimensions of their organisations.

Additionally, the renewed interest in architecture that has been fuelled by the success of large projects, mentioned above, together with more media coverage of architecture and increased access to European cities, has created a more grass-roots demand for design in everyday settings. In response, and partly as a result of the current debate questioning the traditional role of the architect, young practitioners have begun to defy traditional disciplinary boundaries to work in new design and design-related areas. Architectural practices with names like Shed, Softroom and Foreign Office operate variously, both alone and in collaboration with others, as developers, installation art designers, shop and restaurant designers, product designers, web designers, component designers, chefs, television presenters, film makers and so on. This weakening of professional boundaries has also been allied with a freeing from the ideological constraints and stylistic dogmas of the twentieth century and has resulted in a huge diversity of designs, both in form and style, each solution now being able to respond directly to the specificities of the particular culture in which it is set. Design and architecture are now permeating into the everyday activities of everyone, and as a result, making our lives richer and more enjoyable.

However, if the above paints a contemporary picture of a renaissance for architects and architecture it belies some of the more difficult challenges ahead. There is little doubt that the new large and complex methods of building procurement favoured by the government, such as the Private Funding Initiative and Partnering for large projects such as hospitals and schools, are presenting new challenges to the profession. The profession urgently needs to adjust its demography to produce more large practices, improve its management, teamwork and communication skills, and extend its specialised skills, as well as to be able to argue for the value of design in quantitative terms, if it is to hold its ground as a key member of the construction team. These are challenges that require a dynamic response that architects, as reflective practitioners, should be well equipped to tackle.

In conclusion, after the low point in the late twentieth century, the practice of architecture has begun to reassert its value to society. During the last decade, architecture has successfully proved that it can reflect the society that builds it, but it also has the potential to affect the way that society develops. Architects have shown that, by employing their creative skills, they have a unique contribution to make to economic, social, cultural and environmental sustainability and, as such, are invaluable members of society.

▶ 4.2 Building and construction management

4.2.1 Building

While much of the information in section 4.2.2 relating to construction management is also relevant for those studying building, it is illuminating to highlight briefly the different emphasis of building. Building is more focused upon the technical aspect of construction than is construction management. For building, measurement is important, both in relation to quantities but also in relation to costs.

Builders should be able to produce and interpret sketches and drawings, using both traditional and computer-aided methods. In addition to the building shell, building students need to understand the various building services, including water, heating and ventilation, electricity and their place in the built structure.

Building sites are inherently dangerous places where, without due care and attention, accident and injury can easily befall the workforce. For this reason, health and safety issues form a key element of the curriculum. In addition, the legal framework is important to building, as it is to construction management. While interested in the physical construction of buildings, building studies also encompass an interest in their maintenance and management after completion.

Finally, as building forms an integral part of the property life cycle, the place of building and its interactions with customers and other built-environment professionals also forms an important element of the curriculum.

4.2.2 Construction management

Construction management, as distinct from building, is concerned with the principles of management, especially those of project management, and their application to the construction of buildings. The construction process is viewed as a project, the management of which should be holistic from its inception until the point of completion.

Part of the curriculum for professionally accredited courses emanates from the guidance issued as to the generic learning outcomes that all cognate graduates should attain during their programme of study. While some of these generic learning outcomes relate to the acquisition of the skills discussed in Chapter 7, others are specifically oriented towards the content of the curriculum. For example, students should have learnt about sustainability, in particular in terms of ethics, energy conservation and environmental protection. They should also learn about the context within which construction professionals work, including health and safety legislation, quality and standards, and basic construction law. In addition they should be aware of the inherent conflicts they will meet in practice and how to approach the problem of their reconciliation: for example, dealing with the often divergent objectives associated with design and cost (Construction Industry Board, 1998).

So, the programme of study will cover a range of construction-related subjects and skills. Subjects may include the following areas:

- *Building services*, which are the lifeblood of a building and therefore crucial. Such services include provision of adequate light levels for the building's function; ventilation; heating and cooling; and the provision of water and its drainage.

- *Construction technology*, which will include learning about the methods of construction and materials utilised in the construction of both new and existing buildings, for both commercial and residential use. This includes the circumstances in which one method of construction or material is preferable to the available alternatives, and the relevant cost constraints. At the more detailed level, the available choice of materials for the construction of the components of a building, such as its walls and roof, and the relative merits of different building materials and finishes in different contexts and for different building functions, will be covered.

- *Environmental impact* of buildings, including current good practice with respect to design and construction materials, and techniques that minimise undesirable, and maximise desirable, environmental impact. One example would be maximising the thermal efficiency of a proposed building, taking advantage of the natural geographic characteristics of the site and minimising the need for artificial control of its internal temperature.

- *Management*, which will cover the basic management functions, including skills such as communication and team-building discussed in Chapter 7, but also attention to considerations of time, cost and quality, as these are important to the effective management of the construction process. Within this, construction students will learn about the main methods of building procurement.

- *Property surveys*, so that students learn how to recognise the symptoms of structural defects and understand their underlying cause.

- *An introduction to property/facilities management*, which is covered in greater detail in section 4.4.1 in this chapter.

- *Project management*, which involves planning and scheduling the project from inception to completion; procuring, or supervising the procurement of, the goods and services needed to take the project forward; and monitoring and controlling the project during its implementation and at completion. Much of the project management work associated with a new building, or group of buildings, takes place before construction begins. As we have seen when looking at property development, the construction process only begins after the architectural design of the building has been completed, any necessary planning permissions have been obtained, the construction contractor has been selected and relevant legal contract(s) are agreed and completed.

As noted at the beginning of this section, management is important to construction managers. A good construction project manager will be able to:

- act as a single point of contact both for the client and also for suppliers, so enhancing communication and also resolving any disputes that may arise during the life of the project;
- provide existing specialist experience of project management to the benefit of the client;
- advise on costs and on how to keep the project running on schedule;
- minimise the client's risk by application of experience and appropriate risk-management techniques;
- manage any modifications to the project during its implementation.

The management of costs is also an important element of construction management, as the client's costs should be kept to a minimum. The main costs associated with a building can be divided into the capital costs of construction plus the current costs of running and maintaining the building during its useful life. Techniques are available to estimate the costs of a building over its life cycle from inception to demolition, but there are complications to such life-cycle costing of buildings. For example, buildings are normally constructed to last for a long time and yet future costs must be uncertain and therefore difficult to estimate. Costs are also affected by the nature of the building's development. Where clients have given instructions for the construction of the building for their own future use, the capital costs of construction and the later running costs will be paid by the client. However, where a building is constructed on behalf of a property developer who plans to sell the building to a future client, the developer may be inclined to reduce the capital costs and take less trouble to minimise the future running costs, which will be paid by the future occupier of the premises. (This further illustrates the inter-relationships between built-environment professionals in the cycle of construction, development and use of buildings.)

In addition, building and construction management students are likely to be introduced to some economics and planning. Some specialist law is also relevant, including the statutory framework within which construction takes place, and the Law of Contract, as students need to understand the main forms of building contract that they will meet in practice.

Construction managers need to enjoy teamwork as they do not work in isolation. For example, on a reasonably large-scale project, a construction manager is likely to work in a team of built-environmental professionals including at least an architect, a quantity surveyor, and structural engineers.

▶ 4.3 Planning

Sometimes referred to as 'Town and Country Planning' or 'land use planning', spatial planning deals with the making of place and the mediation of space. Planning education therefore should 'promote critical thinking about space and place as the basis for action or intervention' (RTPI, 2003).

> Planners regard themselves as experts at shaping our surroundings. But it may be that the use we make of our land and the design of our built environment are not matters of expertise but matters of opinion, of values rather than facts, in short they are political.   (Blowers, 1986, p. 84)

Because spatial planning can be argued to be political and inherently involves intervention in the unfettered operation of the market, the process of planning is primarily the province of the public, as distinct from the private, sector. Planning is accordingly undertaken by government, whether predominantly at the national, regional or local level, or through some combination of these. The overarching aims of the planning system differ according to time and place: for example, the current UK government's planning aims could be summarised as seeking the attainment of sustainable development through mixed land use and appropriate design. These aims are then reflected in a number of related policy objectives in relation to industry, land use and transport, housing, city centres, and rural areas, and also to special dedicated objectives such as historic conservation and promoting access.

Planning courses will typically consider the following aspects.

- The history of urban planning: how current planning has evolved from the past; the lessons from the past that can inform current planning practice.
- The process by which planning policies are drawn up, articulated and implemented.

- The effects of quantitative planning controls, including zoning, upon real estate development; and the influence of planning legislation upon the nature of that development.
- Planning to control the quality of development through the sustainability agenda, and aesthetic control.
- The process through which application for a development is considered and the criteria underpinning the decision as to whether or not to permit that development.
- Planning control for specific goals, for example, to conserve heritage or sensitive landscapes.
- Planning theory, including the rational planning model, which views the planner essentially as an objective technocrat, and theories that analyse the nature of planning and the role of the planner within the context of society.

There are broad areas of specialisation that can be followed within spatial planning. Urban design, which deals in particular with the interface between architecture and planning in the design of cities, is of interest to planning students who wish to develop their creative skills, and is considered more fully in section 4.3.2. Regeneration is relevant for students with an interest in the development process and the interface between planning and real estate, and focuses upon the effective regeneration of run-down spatial areas, whether rural or urban. There are several variations on the theme of environmental management as a specialism: this is of interest to students with a particular interest in sustainability issues.

Government legislation, in the UK backed up by Planning Policy Statements (PPSs), articulates government policies on the different aspects of planning. The planning framework and its associated legislation evolves to reflect social objectives with respect to such fundamental priorities as supporting economic growth, providing adequate housing to meet the needs of a changing population, protecting the natural environment and attaining sustainability.

In the short term, some of these objectives may not always be mutually compatible: for example, economic growth may indicate different planning decisions from those indicated by an emphasis upon sustainability. Judgement is therefore required by planners and so their job is not solely prescriptive.

As noted earlier, the balance of planning responsibility between central and local government varies between different countries. However, the principles are likely to be similar in that central government legislation provides a framework within which local government authorities prepare and implement their local land-use plans and take the associated planning decisions.

The national legislative framework will also provide a basis for individual planning decisions.

Planners are therefore involved with the planning framework, within which the built environment is developed through a number of stages, from a blank piece of paper – 'the drawing board' – through to the monitoring of a plan following its implementation. The early stages of the planning process are therefore highly conceptual. Implementation and monitoring are the more practical aspects of the process and bring the planner into direct contact with their community. Overall, spatial planning considers how the quality of place and the organisation of space can be enhanced in order to benefit both people and the society within which they live.

The altered emphasis from the role of the planner as technocrat to the role of the planner as a facilitator in their community operating within the current socio-political framework is reflected in the altered priorities expected of graduates by employers. For example, the importance of communication skills to planning employers has increased in recent years, while less emphasis is placed upon traditional design or mapping competencies.

The context of change described below also makes the acquisition of skills, such as communication skills and team working, as well as knowledge, important for today's planning graduate. Because planners are called upon to judge real estate development proposals, an understanding of the real estate development process and its financing is also relevant. Finally, in relation to programme content, trends such as the role of public–private-sector partnerships in the development process and in housing provision mean that knowledge of management skills is useful to the planning graduates both for their personal career development but also for their future work with private-sector or quasi-private-sector clients.

4.3.1 Planning

A specialist perspective from Mike Stubbs

It is an exciting and challenging time to be a student of the built environment generally and of planning and development in particular. Sustainability encapsulates this challenge. It is reflected in statements of national planning policy and in research work. It constitutes the key objective for the system and it binds many policy areas.

Sustainability, as a distinct discipline or component of town planning, is only some 15 years old. The 1987 World Commission on Environment and Development (The Brundtland Commission) provided the first and still most enduring definition as 'Development that meets the needs of the present without compromising the ability of future generations to meet their own needs.'

Sometimes this is rather neatly encapsulated as 'making less last for longer' (RICS Foundation, 2002). While recent research by the RICS Foundation (ibid.) reveals considerable disagreement over how to measure sustainability, there is overwhelming scientific and demographic evidence in favour of action now. Statistical evidence is compelling. For example, by 2030, the United Nations has estimated that 60 per cent of the world's population will live in cities (United Nations, 2001). In England today 90 per cent (or 47 million) of the population live in urban areas, accounting for 91 per cent of total economic output and 89 per cent of all employment. Government land-use change statistics reveal that during the 1990s, England's urban area grew by 0.29 per cent annually. This statistic may appear of little consequence until you convert it into hectares, amounting to 39,000 lost from rural to urban use annually. In response, Rogers and Power have considered the implications for planning to deliver future housing need:

> We know that in this country [England] alone we may have to accommodate nearly four million extra households over the next twenty years . . . we can sprawl further round the edges of existing suburbs in predominantly single-person households or we can make cities worth living in for those who like cities but do not like what we are doing to them.   (Rogers and Power, 2000)

How best to create procedural systems that will deliver a renaissance of our urban areas

In December 2001 the UK government's Secretary of State for Transport, Local Government and the Regions announced a major review of the planning system in England and Wales. The current system was considered to be 'complex, remote, hard to understand and difficult to access' (DTLR, 2001). While the Secretary of State upheld the guiding principles of good planning, he felt that the present-day system was failing to deliver this in that it was slow, obscure at times and, notwithstanding much formal consultation with the public, it failed to engage communities, leaving them disempowered. Such criticisms were directed at achieving fundamental structural change. Yet, the government was not proposing to alter the principal foundation of the system, namely that it involves the public (i.e. State) regulation of private property interests. As such, the government implicitly rejected the case for private land-use planning but argued that many principles built up since 1947 needed drastic review. The Secretary of State felt that the public needed to be more engaged in the process.

The government set out, in the 2001 Green Paper, to make the system more open and engaging to the public, flexible in production of local planning policy and faster in the speed of determining planning applications. A new ethical framework, governing the conduct of councillors, was put in place in May 2002 and a 'Best Value' regime was established in April 2000 seeking continuous service improvement.

Town planning today: rationale and philosophy for change

Today, the land-use planning system faces many challenges. Since the publication of the 2001 Green Paper it has become evident that the 'system', i.e. the procedures involved in the determination of an application, will be the subject of much change in the next few years. Alongside this the sustainability policies that the system is vested to deliver are themselves rapidly changing to accommodate a more sustainable agenda. In providing an introduction to the underlying philosophy guiding the system, both policies and procedures will be considered.

In policy matters, the most significant issue has been the promotion of an 'urban renaissance'. This aspiration is by no means an easy one. Past drift away from urban areas (especially amongst more affluent groups through suburban housing and out-of-town retailing) must be reversed, standards of urban development and design must be improved and the private sector must be encouraged (and supported) to recycle urban land, which may be derelict, vacant and even contaminated. The Urban Task Force grappled with the government's target that over the period 1996 to 2021, 3.8 million new homes would be required, a product of increasing numbers of single-person households coupled with a population drift away from urban areas. If this volume of new homes were constructed on the same density model as achieved in the 1990s, then an additional urban area the size of the West Midlands conurbation would be built in two decades. Such an option would be not only environmentally unacceptable but politically damaging as local people expressed their fury at the ballot box. Further, the Urban Task Force was aware that 700,000 homes were empty in England in 2000–2, of which 250,000 were vacant for in excess of one year.

The Urban Task Force gave a great deal of consideration to the physical and urban design means by which the planning system may repair the city. Four issues were identified for consideration.

First, that past reliance on rigid planning standards stifled creativity. Adherence to highway standards (such as road widths, and radii and visibility at junctions) predominates in post-war urban layouts and this 'roads first, houses later' priority produced bland civic design. Streets should be seen as places and not transport corridors.

Secondly, the Urban Task Force promoted the notion of a 'compact city', to foster both sustainability and urban quality. Sustainability would be achieved by linking urban density to a hierarchy of urban centres/local hubs, providing shops and services within well-connected public transport and walking routes. An appropriate integration of density and the 'connected Compact City' would reduce the reliance on the motorcar.

Thirdly, it should be acknowledged that density alone is not an indicator of urban quality but is an important factor. The Urban Task Force argued that higher densities (and not necessarily high-rise developments) contribute to urban sustainability. Previously, in England one half of all land used for housing has been at prevailing densities of 20 or fewer dwellings per hectare, equating to 54 per cent of all land used providing just a quarter of all housing units completed. Not only is this form of housing highly inefficient but it is no longer a viable means of providing housing when confronted with the dual priorities of satisfying 3.8 million units while stemming the annual flow of people who continue to leave urban areas.

Finally, greater attention is required to enhance urban design, to facilitate mixed-use/mixed-tenure development and to foster sustainability. Good urban design will repair past mistakes and make cities more attractive places in which to live.

A year after the Urban Task Force reported its findings, the government issued an Urban White Paper (DETR, 2000) that laid down a vast array of policy initiatives dealing with the social, economic and environmental dimensions of urban life. The government took forward many ideas, for example to promote the recycling of urban land and improve urban design and architecture. New thinking was emerging in many quarters, ranging across the private sector, regeneration agencies and the research community.

The planning system

The modern UK planning system is a post-war invention, with roots that may be traced to the legislative enactment of the Town and

Country Planning Act 1947, albeit that the notion of 'planning' land use goes back further still, to the late Victorian period in England. Through the planning system, society affords a measure of regulatory control to the government to supervise the use of land. What best distinguishes the UK's 1947 legislation is its scope, principally that it establishes a comprehensive and universal system of land-use control. Then, as now, the system served the key function of balancing public and private interests. The government effectively nationalised the right of private individuals to develop land by introducing the need for planning consent, but, in return, gave them the automatic right of appeal to an independent professional should consent be refused. This newly created system of town and country planning sought to secure the interests of the community, in cases where amenity would be harmed.

The public interest would, therefore, take precedence over the private right to develop land. Nevertheless, that private interest should not be unduly fettered and in acceptable circumstances various freedoms, such as the right to extend a dwelling within certain tolerances, would be exempt from planning regulations. Today, such freedoms from the need for planning permission are granted by subordinate (i.e. laid before Parliament) legislation, such as contained in the General Permitted Development Order and Use Classes Order, which permit certain building works and changes of use without planning permission.

What has changed since 1947 is the policy outcomes that the system is designed to secure. In 1947 this meant post-war reconstruction. In the first decade of the twenty-first century, it means sustainable development so that, by way of example, government policy seeks that, by 2008, 60 per cent of new housing will be built on brownfield (that is, previously developed) land or by conversion of the existing housing stock. In 1999, the government-appointed Urban Task Force reported their findings on how best to foster an urban renaissance amongst British cities. One of these findings related to higher education, where the Urban Task Force identified the importance of Built Environment courses in creating interdisciplinary graduates: 'The main emphasis should be on broader-based courses that bring the skills together with a strong emphasis on problem solving and multi-professional teamwork' (Urban Task Force, 1999).

The Urban Task Force viewed studies in property finance, urban design, environmental planning and urban management as being critical to all built-environment education, including planning.

To build in a sustainable way is also viewed as a matter of commercial advantage for the developer, as reinforced by the RICS Foundation (2002). A new policy agenda has therefore emerged in town planning directed at achieving both better design and more sustainable development. Over the last four or so years, practitioners have had to assimilate vast quantities of new policy, best-practice documents and research. The challenge ahead is to create a new planning system able to deliver this policy effectively.

Turning to consider procedural matters, the UK's 2001 Green Paper led the way in its blueprint for the future system. A new system of planning obligations will replace the current system of negotiated planning gain, with developers contributing set tariffs towards infrastructure (such as the total or partial cost of a road, school or children's play space necessitated by the development). The government will seek a reduction in the volume of both nationally and locally produced planning policy and will create streamlined Local Development Frameworks that involve more flexible (by virtue of being frequently updated) statements of local planning policy objectives. These will replace the somewhat cumbersome current system of Structure/Local/Unitary Development Plans produced by local authorities since the early 1990s. It is intended that the speed of processing planning applications will be increased as fewer applications go before the elected planning committee for their deliberation.

Conversely, the public will become more involved as 'stakeholders', as new participation techniques are introduced. One of these, 'Planning for Real', seeks greater community involvement in the design of schemes. The principal objective is that people are more engaged in the formulation of projects or development proposals and feel less cut off from the system. The existing model involves the public in that they are principally 'consulted' on a planning application – i.e. they are permitted to respond to advertisements about a planning application. This provides them with one solitary avenue for voicing opposition for consideration by the planning committee. Certain initiatives by bodies like the Prince's Foundation (2000) and a number of local authorities have set out to enable the public to become more 'proactive' in their dealings with the system. Yet, the government's aspiration that fewer applications go before the locally elected planning committee, to save time, instead being determined by the chief planning officer alone, is arguably contrary to the principles of participatory democracy.

It is often ignored that the planning system is built on a democratic base. The self-regulation of this base has just experienced a radical overhaul with the introduction of a new ethical code of conduct governing councillors' behaviour. Nevertheless, it remains one of the key features of the system, that local politicians preside over local decision making, even if they are guided by the technical advice of the professionally qualified chief planning officer. As new procedures are introduced, notably the 1998 Human Rights Act, then any reforms to 'streamline' decision making by diminishing this democratic right may collide with such legislative protection. Finally, Planning Legislation is also in line for reform: two examples being revision of the Use Classes Order and General Permitted Development Order, both of which provide an array of freedoms from the need to submit a planning application in cases where such development would not harm the amenity of neighbours or the wider environment generally.

Changes to the UK planning system have therefore been recently introduced, or are in the pipeline or are anticipated within the next few years. The ultimate goal must be the implementation of sustainability within a more streamlined but possibly less democratic system. The student and practitioner alike are presented with many challenges, ranging from keeping abreast of new documents to monitoring their implementation. This change can be formidable but it presents many exciting opportunities for the system, for the practitioner and for the student in the years ahead.

4.3.2 Urban design

Urban design encompasses the study of the relationships between the built and unbuilt environment: the spaces between buildings; the interactions and relationships between one area within a town or city and the other areas that comprise the town or city. The townscape is influenced by the spatial and visual relationships between buildings and the spaces between the buildings that affect the pattern of the streets, vistas and light penetration. The pattern of built space relative to unbuilt space such as open squares and parks; the patterns of light and shade; diversity or monotony of colour, all affect the townscape.

As well as the static townscape, the patterns of movement it generates are pertinent to urban design. The town and its buildings need to be accessible. The need for accessibility generates movement that may flow easily or may result in congestion. (Congestion need not be confined to motor cars in urban areas: metro systems become congested at peak times, and London's Oxford Street can be congested by pedestrians.)

The buildings that constitute a city are the product of urban design – or of its absence! Urban designers need to understand the processes that underlie urban development and the impact of design upon society. The public role of buildings and the spaces between buildings is an important element of urban design: Who will use the buildings and the space between the buildings? What are the needs of users of public buildings and public spaces? Are these needs conflicting or compatible? How can they best be met? What is meant by the term 'design policy'? How does implementation of design policy have an impact upon the townscape and its users?

In addition to the visual aspects of design, the financial and economic aspects of urban design are germane. Urban development has costs in the short term, including the obvious costs of materials, labour and the finance necessary to fund the translation of the design into buildings. In addition, there are longer-term costs associated with the longevity of building materials, security and accessibility. A design with a lower immediate cost may have higher longer-term maintenance costs implicit in it. The professional urban designer therefore requires some understanding of the financial implications of alternative design possibilities.

Urban design involves visualisation of the townscape at different levels of aggregation: What will an individual building look like when it is built? What will its impact be upon the street and the locality? How will it affect the wider community and townscape? In parallel, urban designers must be familiar with planning at different levels of aggregation, from the individual site, to the street and local plan, to the city masterplan. The formulation, implementation and monitoring of plans and the planning process are accordingly all relevant to urban design.

Urban design is a specialism within its own right under the built-environment umbrella: in the wider context of the core subjects considered in this book, it may be best viewed as lying between architecture and planning, with strong interconnections with both.

Good urban design will complement the pattern of activity within the urban boundary and lay the foundation for its future development: it therefore requires understanding and imagination as to the possible futures for the urban space. Good urban design should also enhance the existing tradition and maintain the distinctiveness of the local townscape. A single identical urban design would not be equally successful in every city in the world: sensitivity to existing character and culture recognises that all current development of the built environment adds to the existing development pattern and should seek to do so positively.

▶ 4.4 Real estate management

While surveying emphasises measurement, as the title indicates, real estate or property management emphasises the management aspects of property. The subject is concerned with the utilisation and management of real estate assets, and also with the measurement of their value through valuation. The economic and legal context within which real estate management takes place also forms an important element of the curriculum, as do considerations of wider environmental impact and sustainability. Real estate management and its related specialisms focus upon matters relating to the occupancy and use of property and also the management of that property, both for occupational use and as an investment asset. Occupiers and investors are customers, and so awareness of customers' needs and requirements is important too. Employers surveyed for the Developing Business Skills in Land and Property Management (DEBS) project (www.debs.ac.uk) also stressed the importance of land and property management students having a good understanding of core aspects of business, in particular both the wider business environment within which property transactions occur and also the principles underlying financial accounts. So it will already be clear that the content of the curriculum for courses within land and property management is diverse.

As real estate management education encompasses a wide range of subjects, a wide range of methodologies and a similarly wide range of teaching approaches will be found in cognate courses. For example, consider the wide difference in philosophy and methodology between valuation and law. It is noteworthy that, of the subject disciplines within the Built Environment, land and property management stands out for the absence of published literature and formal discussion of its pedagogy and educational philosophy. In educational terms, real estate management is today still a relatively young subject. The lack of development of its own educational pedagogic philosophy means that it lacks a separate identity as distinct from that of its component educational subject disciplines.

When asked, Real Estate Management students at Oxford Brookes University emphasised the importance of Valuations, Law and Economics as useful subjects in preparing them for their future career. Valuations is often identified as the single subject that distinguishes Real Estate Management from other subjects. To those who enjoy the subject, however, the fact that Valuations is interdependent upon other subject disciplines, in particular Law and Economics, is an inherent part of its interest and attraction. If you are not interested in exploring problems from a number of different angles and perspectives then real estate may not be for you!

4.4.1 Real estate management

A specialist perspective from Peter Dent

No business can operate without some use of real estate and many businesses tie up a considerable amount of their funds in real estate assets. And yet there is still a widespread lack of understanding of the nature and impact of real estate on an organisation's productivity and profit. 'Boardroom ignorance of property issues is staggering, given that outgoings on premises are typically second only to staff costs' (Property in Business editorial, *Chartered Surveyor Monthly*, 2001, p. 1).

The role of the real estate manager or land surveyor has changed considerably over the course of the last three hundred years. By the end of the seventeenth century, 'the land surveyor was diversifying into essential supporting roles in matters of valuing, letting, buying, selling and improving land' (Thompson, 1968). Today not only do we see real estate managers performing these tasks much more frequently, but there is also an expectation that they are equipped with an acute understanding of business as well as the technical skills of 'surveying'. The problem the profession has always had is its identity. Somehow the work of a lawyer or an accountant or an architect is part of the popular culture. But when it comes to defining the role of the surveyor or the real estate manager, the explanation becomes more circumspect and thus often ignored at boardroom level. Yes, a real estate manager will provide valuations, deal with land transactions and advise on development opportunities, but still his or her role is not considered as essential as other professions. Yet, more so than any other profession, surveying has an impact on our everyday life, from our homes to our work to our leisure.

So what is real estate management and who is a real estate manager?

To answer these questions it is necessary to consider real estate from three perspectives. These are the strategic, the tactical and the operational. At the strategic level, real estate management is concerned with 'the formulation and monitoring of real estate strategy so as to achieve overall organisational goals at appropriate levels of cost, thus maximising the value and contribution of real estate to the organisation' (Avis et al., 1993). So, for example, UK retailers are currently seeking to shed freehold and long leasehold ownership in back-to-back 'sale and leaseback' and 'lease and leaseback' deals to raise capital for core business activities. These decisions are strategic corporate decisions which have been taken to meet overall organisational goals. In isolation, freehold ownership of property may be considered to be the best cost-effective option. However, when considered in the light of the business as a whole, releasing capital to supply the core business makes sense to the organisation as a whole.

At the tactical level, management is concerned with converting the strategy into action. This requires the identification of resources and the commitment of those resources to the tasks that go to make up the total activity. An example of this might be the transformation of Arlington Securities in 2003. For 20 years this traditional property company has led the way in UK business park development. In today's climate it sees its future as a fund management and service company with a medium-term aim of floating on the stock market. To achieve this, the company has restructured itself by selling off its property assets into tax-efficient funds and sharing its ownership with the senior management team. In this way it is redefining its asset base so that it becomes an attractive prospect when it is floated. Again, real estate is an important aspect of this transformation. An understanding of the structure of business and the investment market is important to real estate managers so that they can provide sound advice.

Finally, at the operational level, real estate managers are involved in the day-to-day activities necessary to maintain the value of the real estate asset and to ensure that the contractual relationship between the legal interests in the property are met. At this level, 'basic needs will be to carry out such tasks as negotiating lettings on suitable terms, initiating and negotiating rent reviews and lease renewals, overseeing physical maintenance and the enforcement of lease covenants' (Scarrett, 1995). An example of the extent of management can be seen in a recent UK legal case (Theodore Goddard v. Fletcher King Services *Limited* [1997], 32 EG 90). Here a surveyor dealing with a letting checked through a draft lease forwarded to him by his client's solicitor. As requested, and in accordance with good practice, he made various recommendations for alterations. The lease was subsequently amended and returned to the surveyor. This time the surveyor only checked those parts of the lease where he had previously recommended changes. At a later date, it was discovered that the solicitor had also, mistakenly, changed a vital section of the rent review clause that the surveyor had not requested and had not therefore seen on his second reading of the lease. Notwithstanding that the mistake was made by the solicitor, it was held that the surveyor was also negligent, as rent review clauses are of particular relevance to surveyors. This shows the significance of detail and the need to understand what is important and what is less important in terms of overall day-to-day management issues and especially the lease terms that govern real estate activities.

In the Chartered Surveyors Training Trust report 'Business Benchmarking' (June 2000), respondents to a questionnaire identified the need for Chartered Surveyors to have business knowledge and skills 'to understand their clients' businesses so that advice may be given in the strategic context of the objectives of the client's core activity'. In a sense it does not matter at what level a surveyor works (strategic, tactical, operational); he or she needs to understand the needs of the client and the context within which that client operates. The Royal Institution of Chartered Surveyors (RICS) has, over the last few years, been proactive in identifying the significant links between organisations and their real estate needs. In 1998 the then president of the RICS, Richard Lay, set out a four-year plan to bring about radical changes to the way in which the RICS was administered and the priorities for the future of the profession. This plan, 'The Agenda for Change', covered all aspects of surveyors' activities from initial training to employment ethics, lifelong learning and research.

One particular aspect of 'The Agenda for Change' has been 'to reflect the globalisation of property by establishing a new international structure for the profession'. This led in 2002 to the RICS Global Manifesto, which identified the international role of real estate managers. This highlights not only such opportunities as larger markets, international trade, and unlocking new sources of wealth, but also dangers such as the ripple effect, global contagion, and the loss of indigenous cultures. However, the blueprint drawn up by the RICS opened up a vision for all its members. This shows not only the breadth of opportunities for real estate management skills around the world but also the depth in terms of the nature of the work that can be undertaken to satisfy client needs, whether their properties are located in Wapping or Waitangi.

A key question for any organisation with respect to real estate must be whether that real estate, and its management, is appropriately resourced and providing value for money. To answer this, it is useful for the real estate manager to consider the following questions:

- When? Does the organisation currently possess real estate resources and has it adequately planned to have the appropriate real estate resources required to support future business plans?

- What?   What is the profile of the real estate resources in terms of volume, location, value, costs, quality, and intensity of use?
- How?   How should the real estate resources be managed?
- Who?   Who should be responsible for real estate resources? Will it be a team of internal staff members or will it be external contractors and consultants.

'The task of maximising the value that a company gets from its property, whether as an owner-occupier or as a tenant, falls to . . . the strategic property manager. He will have to look at the operational needs of the firm and the physical constraints of the space available in order to:
  a. assess the property costs of the firm; and
  b. minimise the costs of property usage given the needs of the firm.'

(RICS, 2002)

This is particularly so as we move into a new wireless environment. The effective management of real estate worldwide has become a multi-faceted task. Not only should we be considering hot-desking, hotelling, touching down or tele-working but we should also be seeking out creative solutions for energy efficiency, operational effectiveness and financial viability. UK businesses throw away more than £18 billion a year through inefficiency in their use of property. Cutting out this wastage could increase gross trading profits by up to 13 per cent. The skills of real estate managers can provide an immediate contribution to this dynamic and exciting environment.

So, what subjects can you expect to find in the curriculum of a typical Real Estate Management degree programme? While details and the relative emphasis placed upon the different core components of the programme will vary across countries and universities, the Real Estate Management curriculum is likely to look like a variant upon the following core subjects of study:

- Building/Construction
- Economics/Sociology
- Law
- Management/Finance
- Planning/Development
- Valuations/Investment.

As noted earlier, there are some key questions to ask with respect to the delivery of the curriculum before choosing a programme of study, such as: How much opportunity is there to study modules from other subject areas? To what extent are real estate management students offered specialist modules and teaching, and to what extent are they taught alongside students studying other programmes?

4.4.2 Facilities management

Facilities management, as the name suggests, is concerned with the organisation's management of its property, defined as its premises and facilities. At the organisational level, facilities management is concerned with matters such as undertaking and updating audits of exactly what those property facilities are and what condition they are in today. Proactive facilities management helps the organisation to ensure that its premises and facilities support the attainment of the organisation's strategic and operational objectives in a way that is efficient, effective and economic.

A premises audit for a university could lead the university to reflect seriously upon whether it really needs to own and use premises in the expensive area of a city centre or whether it would be preferable to move to lower cost premises, especially if these are more accessible. At the facilities level, an audit will consider whether study spaces are effective, that is, fit for the purpose of delivering courses and supporting students' learning. Some courses require laboratory space while others require large lecture theatres. The audit will also look at the level of space utilisation: are lecture theatres used for as long a day as they could be? Should lectures be held later into the evening in order to increase effective space utilisation? If more students enrol onto a course this year than did so last year, should the course move to a larger lecture theatre or should lectures be repeated in a smaller lecture theatre? Is information technology being used effectively to support students' learning? It may be that fewer lecture theatres would be needed if more study material was made available to students in an electronic format.

Facilities management is also concerned with the purchase, utilisation and disposal of diverse property facilities, from entire heating/air conditioning systems through to light bulbs. There is a large difference between buying light bulbs for a small firm as distinct from obtaining them for a large organisation with 200 properties, such as a multiple retailer. In the latter case, the financial benefits of bulk purchase to the organisation can be considerable. Financial considerations impinge upon most aspects of facilities management. For example, is it preferable to buy the air conditioning system with a higher capital cost and lower running costs or the alternative system with a lower initial capital cost but higher running costs?

Some readers will already be commenting: If the building is a modern one that has been carefully designed and constructed, then it should not require much additional air conditioning or heating anyway! An important aspect of facilities management is to reduce the running costs of property for the organisation. For this reason, it is important that the study of facilities management includes adequate study of environmental issues and of current construction technology so that good practice can be implemented and expenses such as energy costs reduced.

Costs can also be reduced through taking advantage of the available economies of scale that flow from standardisation. For example, the multiple retailer referred to above may use the same architectural design for a number of its stores. This will allow the organisation to save on architectural and construction costs. It will also allow further cost savings as the interior layout of the identical store buildings can also be identical. This saves upon fitting out and furnishing costs as well as enabling the organisation to reap further cost reductions through bulk purchase of furniture and fittings.

The organisation has another decision to make with respect to the management of its property facilities: is this a task that it should undertake itself or should it make use of a specialist facilities management provider? The benefits of specialisation indicate the benefits of using a specialist provider with specific facilities management expertise. However, there are also costs, such as the outsiders' lack of knowledge of how this particular organisation works and the dissipation of internal expertise in this area. The costs and benefits of the options will need to be weighed up carefully before a final decision is taken.

4.4.3 Land management

This book is concerned with the built environment: however, it is worth noting here that a branch of estate management is primarily concerned with the unbuilt environment. While the majority of the world's population live in urban areas, these areas constitute a minor fraction of the land area of the world. A larger fraction of that landmass is utilised for agricultural purposes although agriculture supports a declining proportion of the total population.

Land management focuses upon the management of land rather than the buildings that are built upon the land. Matters to do with the rural economy, agriculture, landscape conservation and environmental management are therefore within the scope of land management.

In many countries the rural economy faces major problems associated with management of the environment, stemming the loss of income and population to urban areas – or both. In order that a rural landscape and its inhabitants can prosper, agriculture and land management need to be sustainable. In this context, sustainability requires:

* conservation of landscapes of natural beauty;
* encouragement and protection of biodiversity;
* encouragement of local food production;
* encouragement of skill development by the population and diversification of the economy.

The latter point is an important one: primary product prices are often unstable or low, leading to rural poverty as in the case of the deleterious results of falling coffee prices upon small coffee farmers in recent years. Economic development typically brings with it shrinkage of the relative importance of agriculture to the country's and the global economy, and so over-dependence upon agriculture is likely to compound rural problems in the absence of diversification. This lesson is not always easily learned: it took the outbreak of foot and mouth disease and its severe economic consequences for the rural economy, in 2001, to point to the relatively minor role of agriculture in the rural economy in the UK.

4.4.4 Property development

The study of property development appeals to those who enjoy a holistic approach to the building life cycle; its practice appeals to those who are prepared to take risks and who have good judgement. Property development is not a risk-free activity!

The process of property development centres upon the financial feasibility of a possible development; its design; its construction; and its sale, preferably at a profit to the developer. Alongside this, property development considers the legal and planning framework within which development takes place, and also relevant contextual issues such as sustainability and how to create sustainable development.

For sound judgements and decisions to be taken, students will learn a range of techniques for financial appraisal and for risk management. Property development is a process with the following main stages.

* Site selection and acquisition.
* Economics of the proposed site.
* Physical feasibility of the site.
* Site development strategy.
* Planning constraints on the development.
* Financial feasibility of the development.

- Design of buildings for the site.
- Obtaining development finance.
- Obtaining planning permission.
- Risk management for the development.
- Contracts and procurement of labour and materials.
- Construction on the site.
- Sale, lease or management of the development.

Property development therefore entails an interest in obtaining, and enjoying a general understanding of, the main disciplines and professions contributing to the development process. The objectives of the interested professions can be inherently incompatible. For example, the objective of commercial property development is to make a profit; the objective of the planning profession is to ensure a socially acceptable and sustainable pattern of land use. The ability to understand each other's viewpoint and to have the skill to negotiate a mutually acceptable outcome is therefore important.

An effective property developer will also have learnt and developed good management skills, including project management and an ability to make well informed choices. The need to work closely with the other actors in the process of development also means that strong team-working skills are essential.

The interdisciplinary nature of property development and the importance of team working mean that this subject is well suited to project work and to synoptic assessments.

▶ 4.5 Surveying

The terminology can become confusing: 'surveying' may be used in a wider sense to encompass land and real estate management. For example, the professional body the Royal Institution of Chartered Surveyors has specialist groups (or Faculties) concerned with the planning and development of property; land and property management; and building surveying. In this case, 'surveying' is used specifically in relation to building surveying and quantity surveying – those professions most associated with issues of measurement and costing in the built environment.

4.5.1 Building surveying

A specialist perspective from Pat Turrell

Building surveying is probably the only subject area within the built environment that encompasses the whole of a building's life cycle, from initial design and development right through to demolition and even to renewal. Caring for buildings throughout their life is one of the main roles of building surveyors, yet they might also develop their career to specialise in one area of building, such as diagnosing defects in buildings or advising clients in historic building conservation measures. Building surveyors need to understand about the physical, functional, economic and legal aspects of buildings of all types. The buildings they are involved with can range from simple domestic buildings, to factory buildings, to multi-storey commercial and complex buildings, and from ancient historic landmarks to futuristic and environmentally sustainable modern designs. Building surveying embraces building conservation, maintenance, aesthetics, law and economics. Yet while building surveying centres on the built environment, the wider issues of society and the natural environment are also key, and the subject area demands considerable personal communication and managerial skills.

Building surveyors can work in many sectors of industry; for example:

- they work for large nationwide multi-disciplinary firms or for small private firms, acting as a consultant for clients needing building advice;
- they work for large corporations and companies with property to care for, and manage their building portfolio requirements;
- they work in the public sector for local and central government agencies in caring and managing the built assets.

The profession is relatively new and is not known significantly outside the UK (apart from Australia and Hong Kong). However, there are signs that this unique holistic view of buildings is gaining recognition, and building surveying is an expanding profession in the USA and in Europe.

Building surveying demands lateral thinking, creativity and problem solving with an ability to assimilate and to understand a wide range of topics and apply them in a practical context in order to achieve a successful result.

The Royal Institution of Chartered Surveyors, as the main professional body for building surveying, has moved towards assessing the capability and competence of entrants at an appropriate level to allow entrance with chartered status. The defined areas of competence for building surveyors relate closely to the subject-specific skills identified as the core components of an undergraduate degree programme. A newly chartered building surveyor will be required to be competent in asset care, development and acquisition, construction design and procurement, building pathology and legal practice. The additional generic areas of competency required of any chartered surveyor, such as business skills and an understanding of professional ethics, are also applicable. However, it is important to recognise that, beyond qualification, the experienced building surveyor will need to develop skills and knowledge through practice and through post-graduate education and training. This is where specialisation in particular areas of expertise becomes more common, such as acting as an expert witness for legal disputes involving building pathology, or developing a specialism in historic building conservation. These areas of expertise demand high levels of competence and the newly qualified building surveyor will merely be a novice practitioner in these sectors of professional development. The scope for later specialisation provides new career directions for individuals to follow and to develop, ensuring a lifelong learning approach.

As globalisation increases, building surveying is being increasingly noticed in more and more parts of the world, in new applications and in new markets. The broader generic social and managerial skills of a building surveyor together with the ability to collect, question and analyse data in solving building problems are appreciated by employers and clients alike.

Building surveying is a vibrant, growing and developing profession. Members of the profession have built their success partly on the ability to be flexible, and have transferable skills that can be adjusted to meet new market needs. The subject-specific skills and knowledge of a building surveyor are both broad and deep. The role of a building surveyor is a demanding one, but it is a role that is tremendously rewarding in its interest and range of activities.

Building surveying is unique in its approach to the whole life of the building. The knowledge of technology, law, economics, building pathology, planning and design, science and management provide a very broad-based curriculum. It is therefore important to integrate this wide range of knowledge and relate it to practice and to a professional context.

The generic skills of building surveying are wide and diverse, and they will vary depending upon the role the building surveyor may take, but will include the following:

- analysing and solving problems;
- surveying, researching and gathering information;
- questioning and critically analysing information;
- all aspects of working in, and leading, a team of people;
- communication: oral, listening, graphic and written;
- being creative and innovative;
- appropriate use of information and communication technology (ICT) and of surveying equipment;
- operating ethically, safely and professionally;
- understanding enterprise and commerce.

The underlying theory provides the important core of building surveying, and the curriculum content continues to diversify as issues within the built environment become more complex. One such example is the growth in awareness of the impact of environmental issues on buildings. Building surveying, with its whole building life cycle interest, has an important part to play in the education of practitioners through sustainable initial design of new buildings, and refurbishment of existing ones; and the recycling and re-use of buildings at the end of their current economic lifespan. The blend of this theoretical knowledge with subject-specific applied knowledge, alongside the broader generic skills required, benefits tremendously from a close link with practice and the professional context. For this reason, learning and teaching strategies that include problem-based learning, active learning and practical projects are regularly utilised to enable students' learning to take place in context. Many education courses will also involve a period of work-based learning where the knowledge is also applied in practice, either through short placements, through sandwich placements or through part-time study routes.

The study of building surveying should therefore create a learning environment that sets the acquisition of theoretical knowledge into a real-life situation, thus encouraging a deeper approach to learning and understanding that can be applied at a later date and in different contexts. This can be illustrated through two examples from a typical undergraduate Building Surveying degree programme:

- Built Environment Life Cycle is often a module studied during the first year of a Building Surveying degree. This type of module aims to make the student aware of the wide range of roles in the industry, but also to give an early understanding of the role of the building surveyor. A field trip to an agricultural building such as a barn, set in a rural environment, provides the student group with a real building to measure and survey. Then, working together in small groups, the students prepare a simple feasibility scheme and present it to a group of clients. The project draws upon simple construction technology, measurement and surveying, and design and communication skills in a real-world scenario, to which first-year students can relate and in which they can enjoy participating.

- By the final year of degree study, an Integrated Project module can draw on real clients with real building problems. The module can enable students to apply their knowledge and skills in real situations under the supervision of academics and practitioners in a safe atmosphere. Examples of suitable projects could include a feasibility scheme for refurbishment of a group of existing houses for a Housing Association, a disabled access audit for the university, and a maintenance survey for local groups, such as a community theatre. In this sort of study, the students form a professional practice, complete with name and corporate image, manage their workload, and are required to reflect upon how well they work together as a group.

Live projects like these also encourage students to develop generic skills. Building surveying requires an ability to relate to, and to work with, people from diverse professions and from diverse backgrounds. As building surveyors work with existing buildings, they predominantly deal with buildings in current use and so must understand the need and concerns of the people within those buildings. This approach is facilitated through common learning with other disciplines, and through project- and case-study-based work that ensures an understanding of client perspectives, social contexts and the particular perspectives of the other members of a design or project team. Thus, at any one time, a building surveyor may have a project team composed of a quantity surveyor, services engineer and structural engineer, plus contractors, to coordinate. At the same time, building surveyors must liaise with planners and building control officials as well as clients and occupiers. Their generic skills are therefore developed alongside, and embedded within, the curriculum to emphasise the relevance of those skills in the professional context.

As the title indicates, the building surveyor has some characteristics in common with both the builder and the surveyor. The building surveyor needs to be able to combine the ability to produce and to use sketches and drawings for buildings with an interest in the functionality of the building. How will the building materials interact and operate together? Will the building services such as water and electricity function effectively? Will the people using the building be able to function safely, comfortably and therefore productively? Like other built-environment professionals, the building surveyor will need to be able to explain technically detailed points both to other professionals and also to building users and clients.

4.5.2 Quantity surveying

The quantity surveyor specialises in providing expert advice with respect to the processes of costing and procurement both before and during the construction process. The quantity surveyor's professional expertise is in the measurement of costs. This entails close liaison with the construction and/or project manager through the process of construction, from the initial planning to design to the procurement of materials to their use during the construction of the building.

The quantity surveyor's role has shifted from being one of measuring and minimising cost to one of more frequently acting in partnership with the other members of the construction team and in partnership with those firms supplying the construction team. This is reflected in a shift from an emphasis upon the objective of minimising cost to that of maximising value.

It is now often recognised that obtaining the lowest price from a supplier may be profitable in the short run, but may not be the best strategy for the longer term. For example, if the price is so low that quality is adversely affected, the maintenance costs for the constructed building may well be higher than would otherwise have been the case. If the price is so low that the supplier becomes unprofitable and goes out of business, the supplying firm may not be available to rectify defects in the early period after the building is completed and this will again add to overall construction costs. In today's world of fast moving technology, very low prices can also make it difficult for firms to invest in new technology. This new technology will usually enhance productivity and, quite probably, reduce costs in the medium term. With these considerations in mind, quantity surveyors now seek best value rather than minimum cost. This longer-term approach to costs is reflected in a more managerial approach to the calculation of costs and prices. It acknowledges that key suppliers play a strategic role in the construction process and therefore may, in some cases, be viewed as partners in that process rather than as adversaries to be fought in order to obtain the cheapest possible inputs to the construction project.

So the role of the quantity surveyor is to advise construction clients, or their managers, on how to obtain best value from spending their construction budget. In order to carry out this function, the quantity surveyor must have a detailed knowledge of the construction process, from building design, through the process of procuring materials, to the actual building construction and its future maintenance. In addition to this knowledge of process, the quantity surveyor needs to know about and understand the cost of materials and their combination within the process of construction: the quantity surveyor will be able to measure, describe and interpret every detail of a building during the process of construction.

The measurement and management aspects of the role combine when it is necessary to predict and model the likely effects of an actual or proposed change upon the cost of a project. Conduct of the cost-control and cost-management aspects of quantity surveying has altered considerably in recent years with the availability of increasingly sophisticated computer software, including spreadsheets and databases. The use of current information technology helps with the task of ensuring that construction projects can be delivered to cost and to time – although experience indicates that, in practice, such perfection is not always achieved. As is the case with building surveying, quantity surveying has also been affected by the increasing globalisation of both the construction industry and its customers.

▶ 4.6 Contextual subjects

In this section of the chapter, we briefly introduce four subjects that often form an element of many more specialist programmes for those studying the built environment: Economics, Law, Management and Sociology.

4.6.1 Economics
Economics contributes to issues relating to the costs of building and also to issues relating to the effects upon the built environment flowing from the spatial distribution of economic activity, and changes over time in that distribution. The pattern of economic activity changes over time: it may become more agglomerated or more dispersed and this density will have implications for the pattern of the built environment. The agglomeration and concentra-

tion of economic activity in selected spatial locations may result in problems concerned with the distribution of income, wealth and employment among people located in different areas. For example, if high productivity, high income and employment in the UK become increasingly concentrated in the south-east area of England around London, then there are economic implications for the property market in the UK, both for the benefiting area around London but also for other less well favoured areas that are not benefiting to the same extent.

Economics is often divided into Microeconomics, which looks at, for example, the price of an individual product or how an individual product is made, as distinct from Macroeconomics, which looks at the operation of the economy as a whole: for example, how much the population spends on all products. This distinction is useful in the context of the built environment.

At the microeconomic level, the determination of price is central. However, while it is easy to find the price of a loaf, of a brick, or of a bicycle, it is often difficult to find the price of some important aspects of the environment. As introduced in Chapter 3, it may be possible to find the price of a tree or of an area of green space in a city – but do those market prices reflect the value to society of the tree or of the green space within an urban environment? How do we find a value for birdsong or for clean air in the city? This distinction between price and value is important to the economics of the built environment.

Microeconomics also looks at production and at the contrast between a country where houses are built on a small scale by individual builders and a country where houses are built on a large scale, predominantly by ten to twelve large companies. The price of land and buildings in the form of rent is also the subject of Microeconomics.

At the macroeconomic level, how the economy as a whole operates and how this affects the property market is crucial. For example, a company will only seek larger office space if its business is expanding. Its business is only likely to expand when the macroeconomy itself is expanding and growing. So to operate effectively in the property market, students need to learn about these inter-relationships and whether the property market tends to grow faster or slower than the economy of which it forms a part. Increasingly, an understanding of global economic issues too is vital – as we have seen elsewhere in this book, issues to do with the built environment are becoming increasingly global.

So the economics of the built environment covers a wide range of economic issues, from the detailed cost information needed in order to understand the economics of building and construction, to the influences upon movements in the world economy that can significantly affect a country's property market.

4.6.2 Law

The law relating to the built environment centres upon several different strands. First, in most countries, ownership of property and/or land is accompanied by a legal title reflected in a legal document in the form of a deed or certificate of ownership. Secondly, there is the law appertaining to the acquisition and disposal of property by owners and occupiers, and the contracts that govern these transactions. Thirdly, there are the legal rights and duties conferred upon both the occupier and the landlord while a property is occupied in exchange for a rental payment. Property, especially commercial property, is often let on leasehold terms. The leaseholder may want to sub-let a portion of the leased property to a different tenant for a short period of time and that can further complicate the legal relationship between the landlord and the tenant. The lease may be for varying lengths of time and the term of the lease itself can affect the likely pattern of occupation of the property. For these reasons, current landlord and tenant law can affect, for example, the valuation of commercial real estate: law is not studied in isolation but in the context of its application to the built environment.

In addition, property professionals need to be aware of current Health and Safety legislation in the country in which they practise. There are also often various forms of environmental legislation that affect the built environment. The legal framework affecting residential property is different but equally important for those wishing to specialise in this aspect of the built environment.

For students of building and construction management in particular, the law as it applies to building control will be relevant. A further strand links the study of the legal framework to the study of planning, because in many countries the planning system is based upon legislation.

For those in Architecture, Construction, Real Estate Management and Surveying, who will be handling the purchase and supply of goods and services on a construction site or for a managed property, a knowledge of the legislation relating to the sale and supply of goods and services is required. Equally, where a graduate will be a manager supervising and employing staff, an introduction to current employment legislation will be useful. A more thorough knowledge will be required by some of the professional bodies at later stages in the student's training.

4.6.3 Management

Management skills are covered in a later section in Chapter 7 of this book; here we are concerned with those aspects of the subject matter of management that are most pertinent to built-environment professionals. At the level of generic management, these include accounts, competition, taxation and marketing.

At a minimum, most people need to be able to read a set of published accounts. A property developer will need greater expertise than this minimum, as will many others working with real estate or construction. In these cases, it is important to understand the techniques that underpin the accounts. In addition, cash flow and financial appraisal are often important topics.

All organisations need to understand their market situation in order to survive. Is there tough competition, or are they one of the few players in their market? If the latter, are there likely to be new, competitive organisations entering the market in the near future and so threatening their current dominant market position? Are there opportunities to launch new products or to sell existing products in new markets? All of these considerations affect the organisation's market position both in the present and in the near future.

Property taxation may be raised partly by local or regional government and partly by national government. In most countries, property forms part of the tax base, levied as a charge either upon the asset value of the property or upon the actual or imputed rental income that the property could earn.

Marketing is important to property professionals whether they are working with other people who have responsibility for marketing a major commercial real estate development or they are part of a small group of individuals working together to market their professional services to potential clients. The relative merits of different marketing media in different circumstances and their limitations should be understood, including electronic media, in order to benefit from effective marketing and not waste money upon ineffective marketing tools.

More specifically, an organisation needs to understand the cost and revenue streams associated with the buildings and space within which its activities are carried out. These are usually classified as: financial, including direct costs and tax liabilities; physical, including maintenance costs and obsolescence; and operational, including the utilisation of the premises and user satisfaction with them. Organisations that take their buildings seriously will use established techniques to measure these costs and revenues and so estimate the contribution that the management of their property is making to profitability.

When buildings need to be changed through additional building or refurbishment, the process of building or refurbishment will often be managed by a dedicated project manager. This specific management role within the built environment was considered in more detail earlier in this chapter within section 4.2, on 'Building and construction management'.

4.6.4 Sociology

Sociology is also an important element of the study of the built environment because we need to understand how the built environment relates to the socio-political framework of the country. In addition, the concept of value, as distinct from price, has a social context, as does our study of thematic issues such as globalisation and sustainability.

People are the inhabitants of the built environment and so they are vitally important stakeholders. We need to understand the nature of changes in people's preferences so as to be able to understand and predict changes in the demands made upon the built environment. For example, many countries experience a major population migration away from the countryside and into large urban areas at some point in their economic development. This migration puts pressure upon housing, employment and the infrastructure, such as the water supply, in the receiving urban areas, and can create a major problem of under-utilised and derelict buildings in those rural areas being depleted of population. When an area of decrepit housing in a city is demolished in order to make space for a new office block there are social implications both in terms of what types of buildings are valued by society but also, more directly, in terms of where the displaced population can be housed (at a price that they can afford). These connections mean that there is a strong linkage between the relevant aspects of sociology and of planning (see also, section 4.3 above).

▶ 4.7 Content, context and skills

Most of the material in this chapter has focused upon the content contained within the main subjects that are studied under the umbrella of the Built Environment. In addition, context is important both to understanding specialist subjects and to students' ability to practise effectively in the real world. The contemporary challenges introduced in Chapter 3 offered examples of contextual aspects of the built environment that will both inform, and be informed by, the particular individual subjects that are studied. For example, the increasing globalisation of much built-environment activity and many of the related issues mean that internationalism provides one pertinent example of a broader contextual issue that can positively enrich discipline-based study.

Students also need to understand the relationship between specialist subjects and other subjects in order to be able to operate effectively as members of a project team. The nature of your contribution will depend upon the nature of the project and its component tasks and upon the composition of the team.

In addition, an increasing number of employers prefer graduates to have a grasp of the business context in which built-environment professionals work. Many will also prefer students to have gained at least some understanding of management skills during their programme of study. This brief discussion of the importance of skills such as teamwork and management serves as a useful reminder of the need for education to support students in developing skills to complement their understanding of the subject content. The importance of these complementary skills as a component of academic programmes of study is such that we investigate skills in their own right in Chapter 7.

5 Courses in the Built Environment

> The main Built Environment subjects having been introduced in the previous chapter, this chapter looks at course provision as an aid to those readers considering how to select a built-environment course, either at undergraduate or at postgraduate level.

Before embarking on a course of study it is worth reflecting carefully upon why you want to study. Studying costs money, if only because the time dedicated to study is time that is not available for paid work. You therefore need to be clear as to the benefit that you seek to obtain as a result of your studies. Some thought about the underlying reason for your wish to study should help to illuminate the other important questions of 'What should I study?' and 'Where should I study?'

In the case of Built Environment subjects, students enrolling upon university degree courses are often overwhelmingly clear about their intended future career path. This is not surprising in view of the primarily vocational nature of many of the relevant courses. The foundation of knowledge and experience upon which these career intentions are based can, however, be more variable. For example, a survey of incoming undergraduate students at Oxford Brookes University in 2000 found that 85% of Architecture students, but only 52% of Real Estate Management students, had even a minimal amount of cognate work experience upon which to base their choice of degree programme and career. This absence of work experience is quite surprising among entrants to a course primarily marketed to attract students seeking a professionally accredited degree programme.

Students who are directly seeking a vocational qualification as part of their degree studies need to check that the course is accredited by the relevant professional body. Professional accreditation of courses in the built environment is important, and so it is discussed more fully in section 5.7. In addition, the role of the professional bodies is considered further in Chapter 9.

Students often indicate a positive interest in undertaking further formal work experience as a part of their university study. If this is important to you, then this is an additional feature to be considered in making a choice of course. Think carefully about the relationship between structured work experience and the length of the course. A sandwich course that includes formal work experience will help the student to gain skills that will be valuable when seeking employment in the future – however, a longer course of study means being an impoverished student for a longer period of time!

Potential students who do not have the conventional educational qualifications expected upon entry to a desired course of study should investigate the attitude of the different educational providers to the admission of 'unconventional' students. Many mature students may not have current educational qualifications to a high level, but may compensate for this deficiency in paper qualifications with their existing work experience – or experiential learning. Bear in mind, however, that some of the professional bodies are quite traditional in their approach to entry requirements and may restrict non-conventional entry routes onto their accredited programmes.

Those students who need a bridge to help them across from a current lack of formal qualification to the entry qualifications required for degree study should explore available courses, such as built-environment foundation courses, designed to encourage access onto degree programmes.

▶ 5.1 Courses and competencies

Many new students enrolling on courses have – at that time – a clear view as to their intended career. Architecture students may intend to pursue a career in practice, while real estate management students may envisage themselves in consultancy or alternatively as property developers. The discussion of the main Built Environment subjects in Chapter 4 has, hopefully, helped to clarify the nature and range of these subjects and helped readers to identify those subjects that sound more, or less, attractive in light of their personal interests.

As well as interest, both aptitude and competence contribute to the ease with which someone can study a particular subject, and so this aspect of the different subjects is explored further in this section.

Architects have strong design competencies. Primarily, architects design buildings; however, there are also particular specialisms. For example, landscape architects are especially interested in the spatial relationship between groups of buildings, while interior architects are interested in the design of the inside, as distinct from the outside, of buildings.

The relationship between buildings and the uses to which they are put are the concerns of planners and urban designers. Again there are specialisms: for example, transport planners are interested in the transport infrastructure that supports built-up areas. The work of transport planners complements that of the engineer: civil and structural engineers work to ensure that buildings and infrastructure are constructed so as to be fit for the purpose for which they are intended.

The construction of buildings and infrastructure is the specialism of the construction manager, who typically needs strong project management skills in order to ensure that buildings are completed on time and to specification.

Surveyors also operate with a range of specialist interests: building surveyors and quantity surveyors are interested in measuring quantities, costs and prices. General practice surveyors are primarily concerned with the value of property in the context of its market price.

Project management and financial skills are both important for property developers. Financial capabilities are vital to those working in property investment, managing property as an investment asset.

Property and buildings in the commercial sector need to be managed, as does housing that is not privately owned. There is therefore a range of professional employment allied to the management of property, encompassing residential and commercial property management and facilities management.

Built-environment professionals do not operate in a vacuum: their professional work is carried out for clients and will have an effect upon the quality of the built environment within which we all live. The immediate client may be in the public sector or the private sector; may be an organisation or an individual – however, the work of all built environment professionals affects the community either directly or indirectly. Studying the built-environment is therefore of interest to those people who wish to contribute to the provision of a secure, sustainable built environment for society.

Some professions, such as planners, often work directly with the community; structural engineers may have greater technical skills and have work that involves less direct contact with members of the public. So, in selecting a preferred subject of study, think carefully about the attributes of the employment you wish to pursue in the future and your own aptitudes and competencies. Are you highly creative? Are you interested in working with people? Are you technically competent? Are you comfortable working with numbers?

▶ 5.2 Interprofessionalism and interdisciplinarity

We have already seen the importance of the individual professions working together harmoniously in order to enhance a well designed, sustainable built environment. It is therefore unsurprising that many courses will include themes or modules intended to educate students in the wider context of the built environment for their particular specialism. It is also not surprising that some readers may find the distinctions and categories between the contributing Built Environment subjects used in this book to be slightly different from their own interpretation, as these distinctions are necessarily sometimes fuzzy and variable among different countries and cultures. There is no intention to marginalise certain aspects of the built environment – one classification has been adopted for the purposes of clarity of exposition for this text, but it does not necessarily represent an exclusive approach.

Some professions often lie across distinctions between construction and property: one example would be building surveying, described as a branch of surveying and therefore primarily categorised with land and property, but also described as 'building' and therefore intimately associated with construction.

One aim of this book is to introduce students to a holistic and inclusive approach to the built environment in order to offer a broad landscape within which they can locate their own particular specialism and interests. Introductions to interprofessional working within academic courses will similarly aim to broaden students' experience and perspective beyond the boundary of their defined field of study: as with the present book, the design of such courses will necessarily be prescribed by limits of time and space, resulting in choices and limits upon the material included.

In order to provide some guidance on course selection in relation to the extent and nature of its interprofessionalism, the following paragraphs accordingly outline some of the different characteristics of courses in this respect. Where a course provides positive study experiences that include learning alongside those studying for the other professions, the study experience will be enriched: so too will the student's experience and competence with respect to team-working skills.

This in itself indicates one key distinction between a course and its objectives: is the course/module designed to enhance students' knowledge, their skills, or a combination of skills and knowledge? An interprofessional module may aim to enhance the student's knowledge base across different subject areas; or it may aim to enhance team-working skills; or it may seek to achieve a combination of enhanced knowledge and enhanced skills. At postgraduate level, such modules may also positively encourage the students to reflect upon their own and others' working practice in order to enhance professional practice.

To evaluate the interprofessional education approach within courses of study, the following checklist of characteristics should prove helpful. Building upon Barr's studies of healthcare education in the mid-1990s, key characteristics of the interprofessional aspects of a particular course can be described by assessing which of the following hold true:

- There are independent interprofessional modules, or interprofessional elements that are embedded into other modules.
- These elements are placed early, during, or late in the programme of study.
- Interprofessional aspects are either present throughout the programme of study (more likely for post-experience or continuing professional development (CPD) courses), or limited to selected modules (more likely for undergraduate courses).
- Student learning about interprofessionalism is explicitly related to current parallel experiential learning (more likely for post-experience or CPD courses), or is related to learning about practice (more likely for undergraduate courses).
- The emphasis within interprofessional learning is upon individual learning and assessment, or upon group learning and assessment.
- The emphasis is upon common practice, responsibilities and perspectives, or upon comparative practice, responsibilities and perspectives across the different built-environment professions.

This checklist highlighted points where curriculum design can be expected to be explicitly different for undergraduate and postgraduate programmes. This is unsurprising: the undergraduate is learning about practice, and about current best practice, in order to become equipped to engage with practice following degree training; in contrast, the experienced postgraduates have already engaged with practice and are to be encouraged to reflect upon and constructively criticise that practice experience in order to enhance their future contribution to professional practice.

Some post-experience programmes are deliberately offered in part-time mode so as to enable students to continue to gain practical work experience in parallel with gaining the learning through which to challenge that experience. Where participating students also come from different professions, or from different working environments within a single profession, then the potential gains from exposure to, and discussion of, a wide range of practice and contexts should further enrich the study experience once effectively mediated by those academic staff delivering the programme.

A strength of courses within the built environment is the range and diversity of subjects that can be studied within a specialist professional programme of study. For example, the study of architecture requires the study of design but also of technology; the study of surveying requires the study of valuation but also of law. This diversity provides the student with a genuine intellectual challenge: it also leaves the student well equipped with a wide range of capabilities following the successful completion of their study.

▶ 5.3 Course features and course choice

Once a subject for study has been selected, it is worth investigating the way in which the subject is taught at different universities. If you are interested in a specialist course of study in Architecture, would you prefer to study at a university that offers a broad base of Architecture courses, or one where Architecture is offered alongside strong creative design, or one where the provision has close links to environmental issues?

More generally, there are a number of relevant considerations, including the following:

- Do you hope to specialise within a core single subject of study right from the beginning of the course, or is the possibility of a broader foundation to your study, through, for example, an initial year or semester of study that is shared across several built-environment disciplines, an attractive option?
- Do you want the option of a period of structured work experience within your course of study? Or of foreign travel, or the possibility of a period of study overseas as a component of your mainstream degree? (If any of these, or similar considerations, are important to you, then these considerations will greatly affect your eventual choice.)
- Bearing in mind that choice on professional linked degrees is often constrained, would you prefer a tightly packaged and clearly focused course with little opportunity to choose the different components of your programme of study, or would you prefer a more modular course offering greater choice and flexibility?
- To what extent do you hope to explore contextual subjects such as law or sociology in order to better understand the social or legal framework within which built-environment professionals work?
- Do you want to focus upon your core subject, or would you prefer to develop or enhance other skills such as language, information technology or communications?

Readers will need to think through the extent to which they would like to study a free-standing specialist course of study compared with a course that enables a greater amount of joint working with other subjects outside their specialism. The extent to which study outside the chosen specialist subject will be feasible and/or desirable will in itself depend upon the level and nature of the course of study. For example, undergraduate programmes of study are typically of three years' duration when studied full time. This allows the time for breadth of study to complement depth in investigating a specialist built-environment subject.

Postgraduate courses are typically very different from this model. In the UK, postgraduate Masters programmes in the built environment usually take one of two very distinct formats. Specialist Masters programmes are designed to enable the cognate graduate to obtain much deeper understanding of the subject that formed the core of their undergraduate degree programme. For example, a Masters degree in Planning will build further upon the existing planning knowledge and related skills acquired by the graduate during an undergraduate Planning degree. Because Masters courses of this type are premised upon the aim of offering a depth of expert coverage in the specialist subject area, there is limited scope for interdisciplinary study and working.

In contrast, there are also a number of Masters programmes in the built environment that are specifically designed for non-cognate graduates. These 'conversion' courses are aimed at graduates of a different undergraduate discipline who wish to learn about a specialist subject, usually one directly related to their intended future professional employment. For example, a history or geography graduate who wished to train as a professional chartered surveyor could study a conversion course in Real Estate Management. Such Masters programmes utilise the generic study skills acquired by students during their successful completion of an undergraduate programme of study and enable the students to apply these generic skills in order to move rapidly along the learning curve for their chosen specialist postgraduate subject. These courses are, by their nature, very intensive and therefore they also usually contain only limited scope for broadening study beyond the specialist requirements.

Where courses do offer scope for interdisciplinary study and work, this may take a number of possible formats, of which the following are among the most common:

- A common core module, in which students from a range of built-environment subject specialisms come together to study a common module based around an interdisciplinary theme or issue such as sustainability.
- A common core semester, in which students from different built-environment subject specialisms come together to study several shared interdisciplinary modules. This approach may be particularly beneficial to students who wish to sample, and find out more with regard to, a number of built-environment subject areas before making a commitment to further study in a single specialism.
- Consultancy projects may be used as a vehicle for simulating the real world of professional employment and encouraging students to work together and learn more about each other's chosen specialist professions in the context of a practical interdisciplinary problem.

- Field trips can similarly provide a context within which students can learn together about each other's specialist subjects in relation to the overarching built environment.
- More generally, projects can be designed in a variety of ways so as to be interprofessional and facilitate shared working and study across different professional subject areas.

If you would like to ensure that you learn more about interdisciplinary and interprofessional approaches to working in the built environment through your university study, then try to establish the extent to which the university course(s) that you are considering will enable you to learn about both knowledge and skills in a wider built-environment context.

▶ 5.4 How specialist a course?

What subjects should you expect to study as part of your Built Environment degree and how specialist will it be? Individual courses vary, depending upon the nature of the particular strengths and interests of the academic staff in different university departments; however, the requirements of professional accreditation mean that there is usually a common core of subjects to be studied for the main built-environment subjects. On some professionally accredited courses, the required curriculum is such that there is virtually no choice available to the student. At postgraduate level, there is a clear contrast between the breadth offered by those courses designed to be studied by non-cognate students and the depth of specialism available to cognate postgraduates exploring a chosen specialist topic in much greater detail.

The following paragraphs provide a brief summary with respect to the main subject disciplines in the built environment. For a fuller exposition, readers are referred to the discussion in Chapter 4.

Architecture

Architecture courses are designed around two central themes: those of architectural design, and architectural technology. Design is concerned with the form of the building, while technology is concerned with its functionality. Design is where the students develop their creativity and visual perception, backed up by studies of the theory and history of architecture. Technology focuses upon the construction of buildings, and issues such as their environmental impact. In addition, courses will often include study of the relevant aspects of management.

Building and construction management

The core of Building and Construction courses is centred upon the construction process, including the provision and maintenance of building services; construction technology; the environmental impact of buildings; and building surveys. Another important theme is that of management, whether project management or the management of property and facilities. In addition, studies include contextual subjects such as economics and costs; planning and buildings; construction and contract law.

Planning

Planning is studied in relation to planning theory and its history; the practice of planning, including the planning process; and planning policy and its development. The implications of planning for sustainability and the environment are important, as are issues concerned with urban development and aspects of that development such as transport. The wider political, social and economic context in which planning takes place is also likely to be the subject of study.

Real estate management

The distinctive core of real estate management is the study of valuation and investment appraisal. As the title indicates, management is also important in relation to both asset/portfolio management and the management of property and facilities. Study also covers the design and construction of buildings, including property surveys and the environmental impact of buildings. A further major strand is that of the planning and development of property. In addition, the contextual subjects of economics and accounts, and also law, including contract law and landlord and tenant law, are likely to be covered.

In addition to subject content, many courses are also designed to teach skills such as information technology or research methods. The teaching and learning of these skills may be achieved through separate skills modules or may be embedded in the subject modules. In either case, the fabric of an academic programme of study consists of both content and skills woven together. (The topic of skills and their development is the subject of Chapter 7, later in this book.)

The summary above serves as a reminder that some individual subjects are relatively specific to selected degree courses in the Built Environment while there are other subjects that are common to a number of areas. For example, the amount and depth of design teaching is distinctive to architecture; and valuation is a distinguishing feature of real estate management. On the other hand, an understanding of property law, or of the environmental impact of buildings, is an interest shared across several of the Built Environment subject areas. Thinking about what subject aspects within the built environment are of most interest to them as individuals should help potential students to analyse the programmes of study on offer and help in making a selection that is most appropriate to their individual interests.

Whatever the main choice of subject, you need to consider whether you wish to generalise or to gain more specialist knowledge of a particular aspect. For example, different courses at different institutions are likely to offer opportunities for specialisation in the different types of real estate, such as residential, retail, commercial, leisure or agricultural real estate.

In some universities, subjects of common interest across the built environment are taught to students from a range of Built Environment courses, enabling students on one course to share their studies with students specialising in other areas. In other cases, courses are more specialised, with Construction Economics being taught separately from the Economics of Real Estate. Do not be surprised to find sharing of courses, especially in the earlier stages of study: apart from some of the larger courses, the economics of university teaching necessitates some sharing of modules in order to allow for specialist provision later in the student's programme of study.

In practice, if professional accreditation is less important, the programmes of study that can be followed in the Built Environment need not be so tightly constrained. In addition, at undergraduate level in particular, different subjects can be combined in a joint honours, rather than a single honours, programme. As a result, the range of programme titles available is diverse and varied, as indicated by the – not comprehensive! – list in Table 5.1.

As can be seen from Table 5.1, courses within the Built Environment have many names: but students are relatively unlikely to graduate with a degree that is actually called 'Built Environment'!

5.4.1 Interdisciplinary courses

In addition to interdisciplinary courses solely under the umbrella of the built environment, there are many opportunities to undertake interdisciplinary courses that connect study of the built environment to the study of courses in different areas. Opportunities to develop built-environment studies in a number of different directions arise through the possibilities created both by undergraduate joint-honours degrees and also by some postgraduate courses. In many cases, courses that achieve this extensive breadth of study will not be those courses that directly help the student to qualify for accreditation by one of the professional bodies in the built environment, but this does not diminish their intrinsic interest to many students.

Table 5.1 Programme titles

Architecture Architectural Conservation Architectural Technology Interior Design	*Building* Building Services Engineering Conservation of Historic Buildings Construction Management
Housing Management Housing Policy	*Planning* Planning and Development Leisure Planning Transport Planning
Real Estate Management Real Estate Investment Land Management Facilities Management	*Building Surveying* Quantity Surveying
Business and Construction Business and Real Estate Environmental Management Leisure Management	

Urban Studies and Housing Studies courses connect study of the urban built environment to study of the social sciences, in particular politics, sociology and economics. Environmental Management and Environment Studies provide a positive route through which to connect the built environment to social studies such as geography and politics, but also to the sciences, including biology, chemistry and ecology. Also, at the more technical end of Built Environment studies, construction and architectural technology can be closely connected to structural and civil engineering. Real estate management and planning can also connect to Business and Management courses, and to more specialist aspects of management such as hospitality and tourism.

▶ 5.5 Choice: university and course of study

In some countries, students have no choice of university as it is normal for them to study at the local university. In other countries, many students study away from home and so need to choose their university. In this case, the choice of university is not solely to be determined by 'location, location, location', but location is important. Do you prefer to be in the centre of a city or out in the countryside? Do you prefer to study in city centre buildings that may be a little distance apart, or on a unified campus? If you do have a choice, unless there is a very good reason why this is impossible, it is important to find time to visit a few prospective universities in order to better understand within which type of study environment you will feel most comfortable.

It is also important to read the information that is available from the university in order to make an informed initial selection of possible universities for a chosen programme of study. Potential postgraduate students will be familiar with this type of information but it can be confusing to a potential new student.

Most universities issue a prospectus and this is the starting point for basic information at university level. Sometimes, representative student bodies issue an unofficial alternative to the official prospectus and this can offer a useful alternative perspective. Within the university, there is likely to be a small number of large groupings, often known as Faculties, so that relevant courses will often be within a 'Faculty of the Built Environment'. Information issued by the Faculty will provide an overview of such matters as links with professional bodies and practice, and key research areas that are important to the particular Faculty. These interests will indicate specialist topics that are likely to be available at that university as distinct from other universities. The cognate discipline will often lie within a School or Department within the Faculty: for example, a Department of Planning or School of Architecture. Information issued at this level will be more detailed again with respect to the subject and the particular programmes offered. All programmes then lead to a named award, such as BA Architecture or MSc Construction Management.

In making your course choice, it is information from the Department about a preferred course/programme that is really useful in helping to select a programme of study. Information available at this level will be more detailed than the outline information given in the university prospectus.

In the UK, the government has decided that all programmes should issue similar – and therefore easily comparable – information to potential students about their courses of study. These so-called programme specifications cover both the content and the skills covered by the course on offer, including both subject specific skills, such as design for architecture, and also general skills such as those covered in Chapter 7. In practice, some programme specifications have become so detailed that they may not satisfy the objective of offering potential students simple, comparable information about similar courses at different universities. Where information is very detailed, it may be of more assistance to postgraduate than to undergraduate students.

Students may plan to study in their first language or may intend to study in another language. As is made clear elsewhere in this book, the built-environment professions and the issues with which they deal are increasingly global. Consequently, an increasing proportion of students do not restrict their study to one country but travel in order to improve or to broaden the range of educational possibilities available to them. For example, in many UK universities a significant minority of students report that English is not their first language. This in itself has implications for programme delivery if the study needs of this group of students are to be recognised and met. Readers to whom this is applicable should check whether the course usually accepts a number of students studying outside their first language. Check the level of fluency that will be expected, remembering that degrees utilise an extensive technical vocabulary that will have to be mastered. If a student's determination, commitment and linguistic ability are strong, studying in a second language can be an enriching experience that will enhance future career prospects. But be realistic: attempting to study a language in parallel with studying for a Built Environment degree is difficult and can be too difficult, with deleterious effects upon students' results.

The overall reputation of a university should influence the choice of a course but take care to establish the university's reputation for that particular course of study. A university with a good record of employment for its graduates will help its graduates to develop their own careers.

▶ 5.6 Courses and careers

Economists recognise that education is undertaken from a combination of two motives: for consumption and for investment. In other words, the consumption of education is an enjoyable experience, and so education may be used in a similar way to the other goods that we buy, that is, to provide pleasure and enjoyment from the activity of being educated. On balance, it is certainly to be hoped that, with a careful choice of both course and university, studying will be a pleasant experience. For many students however, the investment aspect of their education is of fundamental importance. Education is an investment designed to enhance the student's future career in terms of both employability and income. Whether for undergraduate or for postgraduate study, whether by a school leaver or a mature student, one reason for giving up work and current earnings in order to undertake education is frequently the goal of enhanced earnings in the future. This investment aspect of education is perhaps especially important in relation to education linked to entry into the professions, as is the case for many Built Environment courses.

So to what extent should the choice of course be influenced by current career aspirations? To what extent is it desirable to specialise in one subject within the built environment? Or is a broader, more interdisciplinary base preferable?

There are two arguments in favour of avoiding over-specialisation when choosing an undergraduate degree. We live in a changing world and with that change come changes in the type of job that employers have to offer. A glance through the pages of a typical university prospectus will indicate courses and careers that did not exist twenty years ago. So it is likely that, in twenty years' time, courses and careers will have changed again. It is partly for this reason that there has been expansion in the universities' provision of specialist postgraduate programmes designed to enable people to re-train and re-equip themselves for different specialisms and jobs during a normal working career.

The second factor to bear in mind is short-term in its impact. Employment, and therefore the availability of jobs in a particular sector of the economy or in a particular profession, can be affected by economic expansion – but also by economic recession. While expansion creates jobs and employment opportunities, recessions limit job opportunities. With a specialist degree, graduates may find that the availability of specialist employment fitted to that degree is limited in a recession.

All economies are subject to some degree of expansion and contraction, commonly referred to as 'economic cycles'. Typically, the property market experiences economic cycles that are more volatile than those experienced by the wider economy. This means that expansion in the economy leads to even greater expansion in the property market and in related areas such as construction and real estate. Conversely, recession in the economy leads to deeper recession in the property and related industries.

These cyclical movements do affect student choice-property related courses in the UK experienced a boom in demand in the late 1980s to accompany the boom in the property market at that time. The ensuing retrenchment in the property market in the early 1990s was promptly accompanied by a marked reduction in applications to many Built Environment courses.

Because some students clearly respond to current economic conditions in making their initial course choice, and a typical undergraduate course will last for a minimum of three years, then student course completion can be seriously out of line with job opportunities. For example, in the late 1990s, there was a shortage of civil engineering graduates in the UK because student numbers fell during the earlier recession, but business for the employers was booming by the time they had completed their studies.

In choosing a course, do not overlook the reputation of the universities with the key employers in the profession. Employment will be easier if you hold a degree from a university with a good reputation in your chosen subject. Reputation is important in the built environment because the specialist employers know the specialist Built Environment courses well and will value graduates from highly rated courses. It is therefore worthwhile to check a university's reputation with regard to indicators such as employability.

Many professional and vocational courses have close links to the relevant industry. Look out for signs of positive interaction with industry, such as the use of work-based projects, site visits and visiting lectures from current practitioners. These links will enhance course delivery and enrich students' understanding of the industry and its employment opportunities.

Chapter 4 focused upon the content of Built Environment courses – but remember that skills are important to a chosen career as well as a knowledge of facts. Employers seek employees with generic, transferable skills, including information technology skills, inter-personal, team-working and communication skills. It is often argued that communication skills are the key to a successful contemporary career. For this reason, skills development as an integral aspect of studying the built environment is discussed in detail in Chapter 7.

Does it matter if you choose a vocational, professionally oriented course of study and then change your mind about your career aspirations later during your studies? Probably not, once you are sensible about how you present the outcomes of your course in terms of your own personal development. Many non-built-environment employers will offer their own in-house training programmes in order to provide job-specific skills to employees. In this respect, your degree is important as an intellectual training, regardless of the particular subject of study.

▶ 5.7 Courses and professional accreditation

Relevant academic courses of study play an important role in the provision of professional education and training, whether in accountancy or architecture, in surveying or teaching. Consequently, education providers are well accustomed to tailoring their provision towards satisfying at least some of the requirements of a specific professional education as well as a more generic academic learning experience.

Where the provision of a course intended to meet the specification of a professional body satisfies the latter's requirements, the course will be formally endorsed by the professional body. Such an endorsement is normally for a fixed period and subject to renewal in order to ensure currency of the professional body's approval.

In most countries, universities also aim to ensure the quality of their courses. This quality assurance may be undertaken through self-regulation by the universities themselves or it may be wholly or partly enforced by a governmental agency. In many cases, the course characteristics that a professional body will scrutinise are the same as, or similar to, those that the education body responsible for quality assurance will investigate.

These course characteristics will affect the student experience and therefore they are briefly outlined here.

For the professions and for the education providers, control of the quality of academic standards is central to ensuring the future value of that education to the student. It is important that an undergraduate or postgraduate degree awarded by one university is equivalent to an undergraduate or postgraduate degree in the same subject awarded by another university. While this statement may appear rather obvious, in practice it is relatively difficult to compare academic standards across universities and very difficult to do so across national boundaries. This is an interesting limitation, given the increasing internationalisation of the professional labour market.

Factors such as the provision of library books, internet access and the qualifications and experience of the academic staff teaching the course are often sought as tangible evidence contributing to the quality of the student's learning and teaching experience. Quality assessment also seeks evidence with respect to active measures designed to enhance the quality of course provision over time. Education is a dynamic and not a static industry: students should not expect to be taught with antique materials!

For the professional bodies, the quality control of the academic awards that they endorse is paramount to the protection of their members and their professional reputation. For this reason, some professional bodies stipulate that certain subjects or aspects of the curriculum must be taught to students in order for a course to be considered for their endorsement. For example, teaching the basic framework of property law is regarded as essential by some built-environment professions in some countries.

The mode of assessment to be found on professionally endorsed courses may also be influenced by the profession's guidelines. Sometimes, a relatively high proportion of assessment by formal examination may be required compared with courses, such as those in the humanities, without comparable direct links to future professional employment. The professional bodies may also seek evidence of professional competence in graduates in terms of their fitness for future practice. In addition, some professional bodies stipulate minimum entry requirements onto the course that they endorse in order to assure themselves of a minimum standard of entry into the profession.

On the positive side, strong links with current professional practice enrich the curriculum, ensuring its relevance to students. Such links also help to ensure students' employability and reduce the height of the ivory tower!

This quick sketch of some of the main characteristics that describe the quality of course provision in relation to professional accreditation should help potential students to prepare for their own visits to higher-education providers. If you do have a choice of future place of study, think in advance about what facilities and what aspects of a course are especially important to you; and so what questions you wish to ask – and to have answered, before you make that important choice of course for your future study

Part Three
Studying, Skills and Assessment

6 Studying the Curriculum

This chapter introduces a group of three chapters that focus upon different aspects of programme delivery. Chapter 6 introduces study of the Built Environment curriculum. Chapter 7 covers the different skills that students are likely to meet and to develop during their Built Environment studies. Chapter 8 focuses upon assessment, explaining the different assessment methods that students may experience during their studies in relation to the preceding explanation of teaching and learning.

▶ 6.1 Professional education

Many students study the built environment as part of their preparation for a career in the built-environment professions. This means that much built environment education is an example of professional education – in contrast to studying history or chemistry, which do not directly lead on to vocational careers. So, what effect does this vocational element have upon the way we study the built environment?

First, this vocational bias means that studying the built environment often deals with the interactions between theory and practice. The importance of this relationship between theory and practice, and of the graduate's ability to understand and work within that relationship, influences much of the approach to study discussed in this chapter. Secondly, it affects the underlying pedagogy of learning and teaching in the Built Environment, which is explained further in section 6.1.2. In addition it has an effect upon the underlying values of learning and teaching in the Built Environment subjects, as explained in section 6.1.1.

6.1.1 Professional values and ethics

No-one would suggest that either students or their academic teachers normally behave unprofessionally or unethically – however, the need to behave in a professional and ethical manner comes into sharper focus in the case of professional education such as that in the Built Environment. Because one of the main aims of education provision in the Built Environment is to prepare students for a professional career, there is an expectation that students will behave in a professional manner when it is appropriate. Professional behaviour reflects an understanding of underlying values and ethics.

How does this affect studying the built environment? The precise way in which professional values are developed will vary between courses and institutions but the following are examples of scenarios most students will find during their studies.

There will be occasions when students make visits to outside organisations as part of their project work and field work. On these occasions they are expected to dress, talk and behave politely and sensibly: that is, in a professional manner. After all, these visits are part of their training for future employment. There is also the consideration that, if students behave badly one year, there will be no invitation forthcoming from the organisation to next year's students!

A second example applies to students taking a professional approach to their own work. For instance, students often have coursework such as reports and essays to hand in for assessment on specified dates during the year. Students will be expected to manage their time in a professional manner so as to submit work on the specified date, unless there is a very good reason for them not to do so. Why is keeping to deadlines so important? If you miss a deadline in professional practice, you may well lose the client and their business. Most students are not tempted to cheat or to plagiarise on their work but – be warned – penalties for such unprofessional behaviour may be rigorously imposed on courses carrying professional accreditation. Unprofessional behaviour on the part of students is, understandably, viewed very poorly by the professional institutions.

Attitudes to what constitutes ethical behaviour vary over time and among the professions. For example, planners and architects may perceive the behaviour of real estate agents and developers as unethical. This difference stems at least in part from differences in viewpoint respecting acceptable behaviour with regard to negotiation and money. Ethical standards may also alter over time. As an example, some time ago in the UK, it was viewed as wholly unacceptable for public-sector employees to engage in any form of post-tender negotiation in order to try to improve the terms of a contractor's competitive bid, because such behaviour might leave the employee exposed to a charge of corruption. Today, post-tender negotiations form an integral and unquestioned step in the procurement process. On a broader canvas, attitudes towards ethical behaviour with respect to the environment have shifted over recent decades as the sustainability debate has risen up the agenda.

Where do such values as honesty, integrity and truthfulness lie in relation to professional behaviour? Pretty high up the list – both in principle and in practice. What happens if someone is dishonest or tells lies? For a start, if someone begins to tell a story, they will have to live with the story and quite probably embellish it. The risk is that covering up the lie will divert professional energy from pursuit of the core business objective and therefore reduce the professional's effectiveness. (This is different from suggesting that a negotiator tell the whole of the true story in the early stages of negotiation: in this context, there is an important distinction between withholding part of the truth until later, and telling lies.)

Secondly, if someone is identified as dishonest, then business clients will be wary of working with them in future. This is the real disincentive to dishonesty: repeat business is usually more profitable and less costly than attracting new business. It is therefore in the professional's own interest to develop a reputation for honesty and trust, which will help to retain customers and attract new clients through positive recommendations from existing clients.

6.1.2 Theory and practice

A review of Chapter 4's explanation of the core curriculum for the different Built Environment subjects will reveal the common theme of delivering the subject curriculum as a preparation for future professional practice. Studying the built environment is about education for future professional practice and this distinguishing feature pervades *how* the Built Environment subjects are studied as well as *what* is studied, separating them from non-vocational subjects such as those in the humanities.

The curriculum to be studied arises from the interplay between the considerations of the study of a subject that is required in order for students to learn the academic knowledge that is the traditional province of university education, and of the study that is required in order for students to complete their course of study ready for employment in professional practice.

Academics in the field of the Built Environment may accordingly advance the theoretical understanding of the specialist subject in order to contribute to their academic community, or they may advance the practice and transfer of knowledge and skills from the universities to their professional community. The benefits of this interchange between the universities and the professional community are discussed more fully in Chapter 9, where the relationship between academic study and professional practice is explored further.

For the purposes of this chapter it is important to stress two points that follow from the above paragraphs. First, different university courses will offer different balances between the academic and practice elements of their Built

Environment courses. Different universities will also undertake different types and amounts of research. Whatever the particular balance at the individual university, there should be a virtuous circle linking professional practice with research and theory, which will both be informed by, and inform, practice. Secondly, the pedagogy of the Built Environment reflects the importance of marrying practice with theory. One important way of achieving this marriage is through the use of learning and teaching methods that facilitate such an interplay. It is for this reason that learning from projects and problems and experiential learning are considered in this chapter and form an important element in studying the Built Environment curriculum.

One great advantage of the built environment from this perspective is that it is always changing: cities expand and contract; the rural economy and the buildings within it change over time; sites are redeveloped; buildings are designed, built and managed. There is accordingly an endless supply of interesting and current projects and problems to be studied.

This emphasis upon the application of theory to practical problems does not make the learning of theory redundant. The theory must be well understood if it is to be applied effectively. For this reason, courses and modules often begin with an emphasis upon theory and then develop their practical application. Students in the early stages of studying the Built Environment curriculum can become impatient at the weight of theory they need to learn when their primary interest is in qualifying for a practical vocational career. For the impatient, the analogy with learning a language may be helpful: remember that you need to learn the vocabulary and the grammar before you can speak the language. Practice in all aspects will then improve your fluency in the language: as it will with respect to the Built Environment subjects.

▶ 6.2 Learning and teaching methods

6.2.1 Modules and hours of study

Different Built Environment subjects have different core curricula and consequently emphasise different teaching methods. For example, in Architecture, students stress the value of the studio culture. The practical experience derived from field work is also valued by Architecture and other Built Environment students. A survey of students at Oxford Brookes University revealed that some teaching methods were viewed as particularly useful, as shown in Table 6.1.

The extent to which Architecture students value the studio culture within programme delivery is not surprising, while both student groups placed a noticeable emphasis upon field work as a valuable component of their programme.

Table 6.1 Teaching methods

Teaching method	Architecture	Real Estate Management
Field work	57%	64%
Studio work	82%	28%
Lectures	41%	50%
Seminars	55%	21%

Table 6.2 Module study

Teaching method	Number of hours in module
Lecture programme	23
Seminar programme	23
Preparation for formative assessment	24
Preparation of summative assessment	40
Independent learning	40
Total hours	**150**

The programme of study for an academic year will comprise a number of courses, often modules, to be studied over the two or three semesters that form the academic year. Sometimes a subject is studied over the length of the academic year; sometimes subjects are studied in more intensive modules within a single semester. There is a significant contrast between these two approaches. For example, if a valuation module is made up of 150 hours of student study time and is spread over the full academic year then the student will be expected to study valuations for about 6 hours each week and will be studying up to five other subjects in parallel. Where a valuation module is studied intensively within a single semester, the student will be expected to study that module for about 12 hours each week and may only be studying two other subjects at the same time. There are advantages and disadvantages to both approaches: again, this arrangement and approach to study may influence the reader's personal choice of where to study.

How might a valuation module be composed in terms of learning and teaching? If we take the 150 hours, then it might be made up as shown in Table 6.2. So a module that was being taught over the full academic year might have one hour's lecture and one hour's seminar timetabled each week during the main semester period. The students would be spending an average of an hour each week preparing material, on which they would receive an indicative or formative assessment that would help them to monitor their personal progress in achieving the module's learning outcomes. A rather larger amount of time is allocated for the preparation of work to be submitted as summative assessment, that is, assessed work that will count towards the student's final mark for the module. Students will also be expected to spend a significant proportion of time, in this case around a quarter of the total time, studying materials relevant to the module on their own. This independent study forms a vital component of higher education and students need to be self-disciplined enough to ensure that they do undertake it and are not tempted to cut back on it. Normally students will find that they are expected to undertake some independent learning at the early stage of a programme of study and that this proportion will increase as they progress further through the programme. Similarly, postgraduate programmes will normally contain greater opportunities for independent study than will undergraduate programmes.

6.2.2 Modules and learning outcomes

A module, or unit of study, consists of a coherent study package designed to enable students to advance their skills and knowledge in a specific manner. After completing their study of the module, the students should know more about the relevant knowledge and skills than they did before undertaking that study. In order to clarify what the student is expected to achieve by the end of the module study, modules may be described in terms of their intended learning outcomes. These describe the learning that should be attained by the student on successful completion of the module.

At an introductory level of study of a new subject, intended learning outcomes may require students to:

- be aware of how key ideas contribute to the study of the subject;
- apply theories to the realm of practice;
- analyse and propose a solution to a specified problem;
- communicate, using a variety of media, either individually or as part of a team.

At a more advanced level, the language of intended learning outcomes will alter, so that students are expected to:

- interpret, analyse and criticise theories, alternative views and designs;
- evaluate the usefulness of theory in relation to practice; or the quality of information and data;
- analyse and propose alternative solutions to a specified problem, discussing their relative merits;

* demonstrate awareness of the limitations of their work;
* draw conclusions based upon synthesis;
* communicate effectively, using appropriate media;
* manage their time effectively.

The specified learning outcomes of a module are also useful as indicators of what is likely to be assessed during study of the module. The module assessment is designed to test whether or not the student has satisfactorily attained the intended learning outcomes. There is therefore a clear connection between learning outcomes and assessment and this connection is discussed further in Chapter 8, on 'Learning and Assessment'.

6.2.3 Timetabled sessions: lectures, seminars and note-taking

Most modules, or units of study, contain a series of lectures that provide an opportunity for academic staff to explain the central ideas and debates surrounding the subject matter of the module to the student group as a whole. The lectures will offer a series of signposts along the route of the module, clearly indicating how the different study components of the module fit together. A lecture series is often closely related to a specified textbook, or to supplementary reading or web-based study materials. In some cases, lecture materials may have been developed so that they are wholly delivered through a set of structured readings or web-materials, with no formal lectures contained in the module.

Whatever the format, it is important that you take your own effective lecture notes, summarising the key points of the lecture in a manner that is useful to you for your own private study afterwards. The act of note-taking involves thinking actively about the content of the lecture and so aids the process of thinking about and understanding the lecture material.

For some modules, lecturers will provide students with some ready-printed notes covering the core material in their lectures. In this case, students' own notes will primarily be confined to the additional information that they need to jot down during the lecture so that the printed notes make sense afterwards. In this case students will need to make some notes of their own in order to put flesh upon the skeletal material provided by the lecturer. After all, lecturers do not provide these materials to make their lectures redundant. They provide them either to ensure that students can listen more effectively to their lecture rather than rapidly writing notes throughout, or to ensure that students receive an accurate copy of detailed technical material from the lecture, rather than risk inaccurate versions being taken away from the lecture contained in students' notes. In both cases, the printed material is designed to support the process of students' learning the material covered in the lecture, rather than to act as a substitute for the lecture.

Some lecturers will encourage questions from the audience during the course of a lecture: others prefer that students keep questions for discussion during smaller group sessions such as seminars. Often, the whole-group lecture is complemented by a series of related smaller-group sessions for students. These seminars, workshops or tutorials offer greater possibilities for student interaction and discussion than does the more formal lecture environment. These smaller group sessions may take a variety of formats. They may be a useful vehicle for reinforcing aspects of the technical material covered in the lecture series, providing a forum for working through a set of specific problems and checking their solutions. Alternatively, they can provide an opportunity for debating ideas derived from the lecture programme or relevant current issues. Either of these objectives may be assisted by the use of case-study materials or problem-based examples of topics covered in the lecture. Alternatively, they may provide a useful context within which skills, as distinct from course content, may be taught and practised in the informality of a smaller student group. For example, seminars can be an appropriate forum for small-group presentations on a particular topic.

Remember that the notes taken and materials received from tutors during timetabled sessions provide much of the basis for independent study. It is then the quantity and quality of resources accumulated by the student during the overall study of the module that acts as the basis upon which to prepare for formal assessment, whether this assessment takes the form of an examination or of coursework. Skeletal and skimpy notes will only provide a slender foundation upon which to build the basis for assessment – and for future study of the subject. (Readers seeking further information about study skills in general are referred to one of the specialist study skills texts, such as Cottrell, 2003.)

6.2.4 Work-based experiential learning
Programmes of study in the Built Environment are primarily vocational, that is, they are designed to prepare the student for cognate employment. For this reason, obtaining work experience prior to entering the labour market is a valuable exercise. Some students obtain work experience because they combine part-time work with part-time study so that they work and study in the built environment in parallel. Many programmes encourage full-time students to obtain work experience, not least through a one-year period of work during their study – a sandwich year – or through the use of an extended period of work as an integral component of the programme. The learning obtained by the student during this period of work is referred to as work-based, or experiential, learning.

Experiential learning can be, and often is, assessed and students can earn academic credit for such learning. Experiential learning is designed to encourage students to reflect upon their personal experience in the work-place; to consider the role that they have played in the employing organisation; and to consider some aspect of the organisation's approach to its function and/or its clients in order to learn effectively from the time in work. (At the extreme, a property-related MBA programme will be largely based upon this type of learning.)

Different students will be working for different employers and so experiential learning is well suited to a student-focused approach to assessment. In other words, rather than all students being assessed in relation to an identical question or the same case study, experiential learning provides a strong basis upon which to build assessment derived from the individual student's separate experience applied to the generic principles learned during the formal programme of study. In order to ensure both that different students' assessment is at the same standard and also that their intended submissions are actually feasible and achievable, assessments based upon individuals' experiential learning is often subject to a formal process of negotiation and approval between the students and their academic tutor.

The form of assessment often comprises a form of reflective diary compiled by the students from their individual experience in the workplace, combined with a formal report upon the topic of investigation, agreed with their academic tutor. Where experiential learning takes the form of a module of study, it often consists of a relatively short but intensive series of lectures prior to, or in the early stages of, the work experience. This will be followed by some tutorial meetings between student and tutor, but the number of these is likely to be constrained by the needs of the workplace.

This constraint means that the use of a virtual discussion group through which students can share their ideas, experiences and questions to the tutor can be particularly valuable. Such asynchronous learning can also be reinforced by effective use of email between the student and the tutor, thereby overcoming any problems of distance between the workplace and the place of formal study.

Because the detail of each student's workplace learning experience is individual, workplace learning may be assessed effectively through the means of a learning contract between the individual student and tutor. In some cases, this contract will involve a third party representing the employer, in the person, for example, of a workplace mentor for the student. Greater detail with respect to learning contracts as a means of assessment is provided in Chapter 8.

When delivered well, experiential learning can form an interesting and different approach to learning for the student and also one that forms a very good part of preparation for future employment.

6.2.5 Learning from the built environment

Students studying the built environment can learn directly from observation of that environment. In the early stages of study, it is useful to have actual field visits or field trips led by academic staff so that students can learn *how* to observe the salient features of their built environment. Later, students can usefully practise these skills independently in addition to practising them within the more structured context of the learning environment. Architecture students find it useful to visit buildings that illustrate particular architectural styles or innovative use of materials. Building and Construction Management students visit construction sites or buildings that have been constructed using specific techniques and materials. Planning students may visit part of an urban area to see how the provision of facilities or infrastructure such as transport relates to the provision and design of the groups of buildings that they serve. Real Estate Management students may visit a town centre to understand better how its precise layout affects the valuation of individual properties sited there.

As the built environment exists around us as a real learning resource, it would be nice to have many field visits during a programme of study. In practice, the number of such visits is constrained both by their potential cost to the student and also by the amount of time it takes to organise a properly structured field visit that effectively contributes to the student's learning experience.

A well structured field visit will be dovetailed into the module so that there will be preparation before the event. This preparatory work may take the form of an orientation lecture and/or of structured reading about the subject and location of the visit. There may be printed or video/web-based material relating to the site being visited, so that buildings and points of interest are highlighted to students in advance. This means that the student knows what to look for during the visit and maximum use can be made of the scarce field-visit time. Following the field visit, students may have an assignment to complete, or seminars may provide the opportunity for reflective discussion of the experience.

Field visits are important as sources of real experience of the built environment, but also as a medium for developing students' powers of observation of the built environment. These observation skills will be useful both during project work and also in professional employment.

6.2.6 Web-based learning

The extent to which programmes of study and their component modules are delivered through the medium of internet-based resources varies significantly between countries and even among higher education institutions within the same country. It is certain that, as a mode of delivery, internet-based learning will increase, both for students learning online at a distance from their home institution and also for students studying at a conventional campus.

At a basic level, a course or module website can be a useful repository for information to which students need to refer. This information can include course handbooks and key references, including linked websites. Sometimes, outline lecture notes and related materials can be loaded onto the website. This material provides a useful resource to which the students can refer, for example, to check a technical point made in a lecture and ensure that their own notes are accurate. This checking mechanism is especially useful for technical detail, where accuracy is vital, such as that found in real estate valuation or construction technology.

In some instances, teaching information on the web can be interactive, as it has to be in the case of online delivery. Interactive teaching materials can also provide exercises that allow the students to work through examples and confirm their understanding of central concepts.

Contact between individual students and their tutors by electronic mail is commonplace. The next step in this context is the use of electronic bulletin boards and discussion groups in order to facilitate contact among the group of students studying the course, and between the tutor and the whole student group. Diversity of means of communication brings additional benefits: for example, experience indicates that introvert students who may find it difficult to contribute orally in a class situation contribute readily to electronic discussion.

The web and internet resources have provided an additional medium for the delivery of learning and teaching and, as such, enrich the possibilities of study. Normally they offer a useful complement to more traditional modes of delivery. They allow for asynchronous contact between student and student, and between student and tutor. The student can send an email at 01.00 a.m., if that is when he or she prefers to study, and the tutor can answer it at 10.00 a.m. A further benefit is that web-based learning allows individual students to study different subjects at their own pace: taking their time over subjects and ideas that they find difficult and spending less time on those aspects of study that they find easy. This ability to tailor the pace of study is of considerable benefit when studying the built environment because the diversity of the subjects studied makes it highly unlikely that the student will be equally competent at all of them.

At the extreme, it is possible to study exclusively through the use of online materials. In this case distance is, literally, no object and the possibilities are global, subject to restrictions such as those imposed by language and the availability of the necessary IT skills and equipment.

6.2.7 Independent learning

It was noted in section 1.1.1 above, that much study time is designed for the student's independent learning. Built Environment students typically do not spend long hours being taught their subjects. Instead they have long hours between sessions with their tutors in which to learn on their own. This independent learning does not have to be a lonely process: informal discussion and exchange of ideas with fellow students can be effective – and also provide reassurance that other students are facing similar difficulties with the module!

Independent learning can take different forms. It may require time spent in reading recommended background material, for a subject such as planning; in working through set problems, for a subject such as valuation; or in design studio work, for architecture. It is important for students to manage their time so as to approach independent learning seriously: students do not succeed by studying during class time alone!

Independent study time also provides opportunities for the thought and reflection that are difficult, if not impossible, while listening and/or writing during contact sessions in a formal class. Check what has been understood and what remains difficult about the subject. Take care to pay attention to the less interesting aspects of the module as well as those elements that are exciting and encouraging your interest in study. Where there are opportunities to answer short questions, undertake brief tests, or answer quizzes, take these opportunities in order to obtain realistic feedback on your progress.

Fellow students are a resource to be drawn upon through informal discussion, and to provide mutual help. The course tutor is also a resource, so make a note of questions to be asked at the next contact session so that difficult points can be clarified.

As students progress through their course, the importance of independent learning increases. After all, for most Built Environment courses, one aim of the course is to educate a future self-motivated professional. For this reason, project work often includes opportunities for independent learning. A major opportunity for independent learning is provided by the extended project or dissertation that forms a major component of final-year undergraduate study and of most postgraduate courses. In view of this importance, the dissertation is covered in the separate section 6.3.

6.2.8 Learning in a group

It was noted above that other students can act as a learning resource and offer support, so that the peer group can be a positive aid to each student's learning. For this reason and also because, in professional practice, teamwork is often more important than individual work, some activities are designed specifically to be undertaken by students as a group rather than as individuals. Depending upon the particular group task, group size may vary from two or three to a larger group of seven or eight. The implications of different sized groups differ. A larger group means that there are more people amongst whom to share the tasks, but if the group is to operate efficiently, there is a much larger coordination task to be carried out than is the case with a smaller group.

Group work can be used for seminar presentations, in which different groups take turns to present to their fellow students. Group work is often also appropriate for a variety of project work.

From the student's viewpoint, working as part of a group has two main advantages. It encourages the development of team-working skills and is closer to professional work in employment than is individual work. Combining the different knowledge and experience of a group of students also enhances the overall learning experience for each individual, because of the positive synergics arising from positive group interaction. In addition, working directly with other students helps them to develop their understanding of people's differing personalities. Importantly, it also helps students to recognise that different people have different learning styles and to observe these different learning styles in action. (A more detailed discussion of how students can tailor their contribution in order to get the maximum benefit from group work is to be found in chapter 5 of Cottrell, 2003.)

There is one drawback to group learning which constrains the extent to which group assessment should be used in any course: successful group work presupposes that all group members are willing and able to make an equivalent contribution to the work carried out by the group. Where an individual student group member fails to participate actively in the group, the benefits of the learning exercise can be significantly undermined. When involved in group work therefore, students should endeavour to ensure that all members of the group are encouraged to be involved and to participate fully. On those occasions when a student is not participating, the academic tutor responsible should be informed as soon as possible. Usually, however, group work is an enjoyable as well as an educational experience for the participants.

6.2.9 Learning from projects and problems

Theory is rarely taught in isolation in the Built Environment subjects. It is more usual for theory and ideas to be taught in relation to the problems and situations in which they can be applied. This emphasis upon real-world applicability means that looking at practical problems and projects plays an important role in the study of the built environment.

The use of project work in learning and teaching allows a topic to be investigated in greater depth and in relation to its practical context. It also facilitates independent enquiry and learning by students, whether working as individuals or as the contributing members of a group. Problems and projects offer flexibility to the teacher in designing the delivery of the curriculum and so can be used as a means of ensuring that students develop a wide variety of knowledge or skills. This diversity is reflected in diversity of approach and of assessment, discussed at greater length in Chapter 8.

Many projects in the built environment encourage students to learn through the analysis and solution of problems. At an introductory level, the nature of problems is usually simplified in comparison with those faced in reality, in order to make the task manageable. As the student develops an understanding of the subject, the problems set become more complex and realistic. Once students are competent, projects set can be based partly or wholly on a real-world 'live' problem. Such problems are usually set by academic tutors in liaison with partners in the profession and the students' solutions are shared with those professional partners and may be commented upon by them. This process is valuable because it allows students to better understand the interplay with clients that they will experience in professional employment.

Such live problems can be applied in all the main subject disciplines in the Built Environment course. Live projects can be formulated based upon the challenges faced by the university in managing its own built environment, whether through a current building design issue; a construction challenge; an aspect of managing its real estate; or a pending planning application.

At more advanced levels of an undergraduate course, or during a postgraduate course, project briefs are designed so as to allow the students some input into the way they interpret and respond to the project brief. This allows the students to direct part of their own learning, rather than leaving them wholly dependent upon direction from their tutor.

Studying through projects and problems is very different from studying solely through a traditional lecture programme supplemented by directed reading of the relevant literature. Undertaking projects and solving problems requires the student to focus upon the learning *process* rather than primarily upon learning knowledge. In relatively simple terms, undertaking a project requires the students to do the following:

- Identify their learning goal – Where am I going?
- Plan their learning activities – How am I going to get there?
- Find and use learning resources – going there.
- Evaluate their learning – Where did I actually go? Could I have done it better?

The closer the project to a real-world scenario, and the greater the students' input into how they interpret and respond to the project brief, the greater is the independent learning and the similarity to professional practice.

A further step towards student-directed independent learning is to allow the students to have an input into the design of the project that they are to pursue. This approach can be facilitated through the mechanism of learning contracts, discussed in Chapter 8. It is also crucial to the success of the largest single project that students undertake as an element of their course: the dissertation.

▶ 6.3 Dissertations

For some undergraduate programmes and most postgraduate programmes, students will be expected to undertake a dissertation as an important course component towards the end of their programme of study. A dissertation is more than an extension of the essay: it is a carefully structured piece of independent work undertaken by the student. (The study skills required for undertaking a dissertation successfully are introduced in Cottrell, 2003, chapter 9.) The usual form for the structure of a dissertation is described in the following parts of this section.

6.3.1 Student-directed learning

From the student's perspective, an important aspect of the dissertation is that it provides a unique opportunity for substantial student-directed learning, as distinct from tutor-directed learning. In some cases, students will be asked to select their dissertation topic from a prescribed list of options; in other cases, there will be greater freedom for students to choose their own topic for investigation once the topic fits sensibly within the framework of the course. The tutor's role in the dissertation is to guide and facilitate, rather than to teach the student. This guidance, based upon the tutor's experience of the course and the subject matter, is very valuable. It is therefore important that students remember to use their dissertation tutor as a resource and to take the opportunities available to seek tutorial guidance while working on the dissertation. The length of a student dissertation usually lies within the range of 8,000 to 20,000 words. Students should expect to be provided with clear guidance as to the length expected, and practical details such as how to reference source material in the body of the written submission.

So, what are the main components of a dissertation and therefore how should students approach the task of undertaking a dissertation? The following sections should provide some generic guidance for this important component of course assessment. First, however, let us look at an important issue that needs to be considered before the dissertation is started.

It has already been noted that a dissertation often comprises a significant element of the final assessment for a programme of study. It is therefore vital for students to ensure that their own project management of the dissertation task as a project in itself is conducted seriously and effectively. How long a period of time has been allocated within which to complete the dissertation? How many hours of student effort are allocated to the dissertation? Read the sections below and begin to understand in more detail the nature of the dissertation task and how it applies to your own circumstances. Then begin to think about how you need to divide your time among the different component parts of the dissertation task in order to complete it within the time allotted. As a tip, most students do not leave enough time for the analysis of their results and for writing their concluding section. These two sections are closely related: should you fail to analyse your results adequately, you will have no adequate basis from which to draw conclusions. A dissertation with a weak analysis will be a dissertation with a weak concluding section.

It will be worthwhile to treat the dissertation as a project in need of project management and to check your time management of the task regularly during the period over which you are working on your dissertation. This may well be a pressured time: you may have other assessments to prepare and/or you may be applying for jobs during the same period. Do not put off your dissertation until the last minute: it is too large a task to be undertaken successfully in a hurry.

6.3.2 Aims and objectives

Before you begin serious work on your dissertation, you will need to have an idea of its subject matter: what will it be about? You will be working on this dissertation for a significant part of your final year of study, and so it is vital that you choose a topic that is both relevant to your course and also of interest to you. A topic that you find interesting will make the difference between an enjoyable and a boring dissertation experience – and, if you find the topic boring, your boredom will be reflected in your final written submission!

What aspects of your course do you enjoy?

What type of employment are you thinking about, following your studies?

You will benefit from identifying a dissertation topic that is relevant to one or the other of these questions, or even relevant to both.

So, what are you going to find out about? Can you turn this topic into a question to be answered?

Once you have this type of question, you have a research question. Remember that it will not matter whether your dissertation research yields the answer 'Yes' or 'No', provided that you undertake the dissertation task properly. Your research question is known as your hypothesis: the primary aim of your dissertation will be to test that hypothesis.

Now think about the nature of the secondary questions, or sub-topics, that you will need to consider in order to achieve your dissertation's aim. These secondary topics are your objectives: their investigation is necessary in order to achieve the aim of the dissertation.

These concepts of hypothesis, aims and objectives will be helpful independent of whether your dissertation primarily takes the form of a literature review (which we refer to as secondary research) or is mainly about undertaking your own research (primary research). Once you have developed some ideas as to what you would like your dissertation to be about in this structured way, talk about your ideas with fellow students and with your tutor. If it is possible, it is also very helpful to discuss your ideas at an early stage with someone actually working in employment in the field relevant to your proposed topic: their perspective will certainly help you to see the practical aspects of the question and whether or not it is currently important to professional practice.

6.3.3 Rationale

Don't worry about the jargon: think about what it means! Before you go any further with the topic that you think you will study for your dissertation, having drafted a hypothesis, aims and objectives, subject the topic to a simple test.

Is it important? Not just important to you, but does it matter to the profession you hope to join? Is it important because it is highly relevant to the subject of your degree programme? Is it interesting – not just to you but also to the subject community?

If the answer to these questions is positive, then you can be reassured and you can also write down why your topic is important: it will be worthwhile to include this rationale in the introductory section of your written dissertation.

If the answer to these questions is persistently, 'perhaps', or 'no', then think again before you spend any more time on a topic that may be of dubious merit. Is there a different perspective on the original topic that would make it more relevant/interesting/important? Talking to other people may help you find such a different perspective. If not, then you probably need to think about an entirely different dissertation topic that will fulfil these criteria and provide you with a firm foundation on which to build your dissertation studies.

6.3.4 Literature review

The breadth and depth of a literature review will depend upon its importance in relation to the overall dissertation task that you have been set. In some cases, the literature review may form the main substance of your dissertation; in other cases, it will provide the context for your own primary research. In all cases, you will need to remember the wide range of literature and literature sources available in the built environment and the different media in which they are likely to be available.

As well as the narrowly specific, your literature review will be about providing context for your argument and so you will also need more general theoretical source materials. If you are researching a specific type of residential housing development, using a particular example in south-east London as a case-study to illustrate your hypothesis, you are unlikely to find direct references to your case-study location on the university library shelves. The library will contain more generic materials concerning the nature of contemporary housing developments and good practice in this respect, which will provide important contextual material for your dissertation. Specific information with regard to your individual case study is more likely to be found in trade and professional journals and magazines. And remember that direct information from the developer is unlikely to be wholly objective: it is likely to be influenced by their desire to utilise published material to enhance their corporate image in the outside world!

In this new century, do not expect to confine your definition of literature to the printed word on the shelf, either: online material is both relevant and accessible and should be used.

Record keeping is an important skill within dissertation preparation. As soon as you begin to read literature relating to your dissertation topic, it is useful to make two relevant records about each item. First, make a note of the appropriate reference so that you can add it later to the Bibliography at the end of your dissertation if it turns out to be relevant and useful, and so that you can cite it in your written dissertation. You should receive guidance as to how to reference your particular dissertation, because there are several accepted forms of referencing and most universities prefer students to be consistent in using a specific format (for example, all references and the bibliography for this book have been prepared using Harvard referencing). Secondly, jot down a note of the key points contained in any materials you read so that you have a note for later use of materials that relate to specific aspects of your topic, and can easily refer back to them should you want to investigate the material in greater depth.

6.3.5 Primary research

In those cases where a dissertation in the Built Environment includes the undertaking of some primary research, you will need to consider how to research your topic, and then how to analyse and interpret the results of your research.

In order to research your topic, you will need to use one or more ways of gathering together the relevant data. These different ways of gathering data are called research methods, and so, how you gather your data is referred to as your research methodology. There are a number of ways of gathering data: through the use of structured questionnaires, through structured interviews, through the use of illustrative case studies or through a combination of these. While the research methodology associated with a PhD thesis is necessarily sophisticated, do not be over-ambitious with primary research for undergraduate and masters programmes: here it is more important to be effective than to be ambitious.

You will need to refer to at least two different textbooks on research methodology in order to decide what method(s) will be appropriate for your own study. Once you have some ideas about what method(s) might be useful and practical for your own research, think about how you would use them in order to gain useful data with which to answer your research question. Now, before you go any further, you are again at a stage where you should consult your tutor for guidance as to whether or not you are going in the right direction: remember, your tutor has more experience than you have!

Once you have gathered your data, you need to consider the results, interpret them and find ways of presenting them in an interesting way within your dissertation. Some courses will expect you to have the skills necessary to undertake statistical manipulation of your data; other courses will expect you to think about and to present the data effectively, using such devices as histograms, or pie-charts, to present your findings. Again, details as to the extent to which you are expected to formally analyse your data should be clear from the instructions provided and the other learning that you have undertaken during your course.

6.3.6 Conclusions

Your research (whether primary, secondary, or a combination of both) should lead you to be able to draw a number of conclusions with respect to your dissertation aims and objectives. In some cases, your work will have clearly yielded a 'yes' or 'no' answer to your research question. In other cases, there may be no clear answer, one way or the other, but your work will have illuminated more clearly the nature of the question. You should also be able to report further conclusions with respect to your secondary objectives.

In writing your conclusions, take care to report also upon the limitations of your dissertation research: you cannot cover everything within the confines of a single dissertation. You may also find it interesting to report upon the further research questions that your current work has pointed up.

Finally, you need to remember that the last word that you write in your conclusion does not complete the task of finishing your dissertation. Is your Bibliography and referencing accurate and complete? Have you included formal acknowledgements to people who have given you help with information for your dissertation? Have you checked your spelling? It would be a pity to cast a shadow upon all your hard work by submitting a dissertation containing basic spelling errors. A professional approach to your work at all times is always a good preparation for your future professional career in the built environment.

7 Learning Skills and Techniques

Studying the built environment is concerned with the acquisition of relevant knowledge and skills. Having looked at studying the curriculum in Chapter 6, we concentrate in this chapter upon those skills most pertinent to studying the built environment.

▶ 7.1 Skills and the curriculum

The skills required for life and employment in the new century are different from those of a hundred years ago. Today the emphasis is on the 'knowledge economy' and upon educating students to have the creative skills that will enable them to act independently, to generate, apply and synthesise new ideas and knowledge. The contemporary 'body of knowledge' is larger, more complex and more dynamic than ever before, requiring different expertise and skills in order to use and manipulate it effectively. As a result, the learning skills that are needed by students are different from, and more complex than, those required by a student a century ago.

For the professional and vocational courses in the Built Environment, both employers and the professional institutions affect the links between skills and other aspects of the curriculum.

- *Employers.* Because courses in the built environment are primarily vocational, the needs of employers and the employability of graduates have an impact upon the curriculum and its delivery. Where employers positively prefer graduates to have the skills and competencies that they will require for professional practice, then a curriculum and delivery modes that foster these skills are more likely to emerge.

- *The professional institution.* Individual university courses are also shaped by the influence of professional bodies such as those cognate to the built environment, and their guidelines with respect to not only curriculum content but also student skills and competencies.

Aspects of a course relevant to the development of student learning skills in the individual module or integrated across the programme of study can be broadly categorised under four subheadings:

- *Curriculum design.* The underlying principles that inform and structure the design of the curriculum can positively facilitate student skill development, as evidenced within the rationale, objectives and learning outcomes.

- *Pedagogy and delivery.* Modes of learning and teaching can promote learning activities that foster and enhance an understanding of skills and competencies.

- *Curriculum content.* Skills can be fostered through a curriculum that includes materials informed by skills, including those relevant to professional practice.

- *Assessment.* The curriculum assessment strategy can be designed so as to assess learning outcomes and student capabilities that monitor and develop student performance with respect to skill development.

7.1.1 The student perspective

When asked which skills they expected to be very useful to them for their intended career, students at Oxford Brookes highlighted those listed in Table 7.1. Both student groups identified information and communication technology as a key skill necessary to their future career. With the exception of ICT, there is a clear distinction between the type of skills identified by Architecture students and those emphasised by the Real Estate Management students. The former emphasised the importance of design and presentation, while the Real Estate Management students highlighted communication, teamwork and management skills. In contrast, teamwork and management were not seen as important by the Architecture students.

Table 7.1 Skills – the student perspective

Skill	Architecture	Real Estate Management
Information technology	35%	42%
Communication	18%	32%
Design	38%	2%
Teamwork	7%	28%
Presentation	22%	8%
Management	0%	26%

These results reflect the essential cultural distinction between architecture and real estate management and are an important consideration for the individual's career choice. Architects tend to spend more time working individually while real estate management is often more concerned with teamwork. In general, architects spend time working creatively while surveyors spend time on management and teamwork. These are sharp contrasts: one example of the diversity and richness across the built environment, and also an example of the importance of pursuing personal interests in an area of the built environment that is consonant with the individual's personality and interests.

7.1.2 The employer perspective

Employers also value graduates for their skills and competencies in addition to their knowledge and – where appropriate – experience. A recent UK research project into Developing Business Skills in Land and Property Management courses (DEBS) surveyed 500 land- and property-management employers. One key result from the research was that these employers valued generic skills in the graduate employees far more than the students' subject-specific skills and knowledge. Students should therefore be prepared to analyse the curriculum in relation to these attributes. Think carefully about what can be gained from a course of study – and also what will be valued by potential future employers.

The most important generic skills identified by those surveying employers studied in the DEBS project were communication skills, identified as essential by over 90 per cent of respondents. In this context, essential communication skills encompassed verbal and aural communication as well as written communication skills. These generic skills help graduates to adapt successfully to the world of work as soon as they enter employment. Once in employment, one necessary condition for career success is a reflective approach to practice, and involvement in continued professional development: the beginnings of such a reflective approach should therefore be seeded in the students during their studies.

To be taught effectively, the skills component of the curriculum needs to be made explicit to students both at the beginning of their study and also at relevant points during their studies; they should be encouraged to undertake reflective practice and should be helped to see the ways in which their learning has applications to their future professional practice. One conclusion the DEBS project members inferred from their results was that undergraduate programmes should concentrate upon teaching students about the subject matter of surveying combined with these generic skills, leaving the subject-specific surveying skills to be acquired at postgraduate level or through structured work experience linked to continued professional development.

▶ 7.2 Personal reflection

We have already noted the fact that many degree programmes in the Built Environment are closely linked to entry into the cognate professions. So the education of many Built Environment students is concerned with preparing the graduates for a professional career in addition to helping them to learn about their chosen subject(s). As part of this inherent professionalism, students are taught how to develop as reflective professionals or reflective practitioners, that is, as people who will take the time and trouble to reflect upon, and evaluate, their practical experiences and to learn from those experiences in the context of their developing professional career.

So how do we help students to develop the techniques of self-reflection and self-learning?

It is often easier to begin to develop these skills within the context of working with peers. In this case, a small group of students may be asked to reflect upon a recent learning experience and to share and discuss their thoughts within the group before sharing their main conclusions with the wider student group and the teacher. This provides a non-judgemental introduction to the idea of self-reflection and critical self-evaluation.

Later, students may be asked to write brief self-evaluative reports upon their preparation of a piece of coursework as an integral component of that coursework. Being assessed upon their skills of personal reflection provides the incentive to take this skill seriously and also to obtain some formal formative feedback upon their performance.

Both of the above examples illustrate cases of discontinuous personal reflection. For personal reflection to become an embedded skill, an activity that is automatically undertaken by the student learning to behave as a future professional at key stages during a project and at its completion, some more continuous form of self-reflection is required. A dedicated file in which the student compiles these records, sometimes known as a progress file, is one means of seeking to achieve this objective.

Some universities will use a common progress-file system for all their students; some students will have begun this process earlier in their educational career and so be familiar with the concept before arriving at university. For all students, the aim is to develop how they use the file and its contents as they progress through their programme of study. The progress file may form the basis for regular conversations with the student's personal tutor or counsellor. Such conversations with a trained professional will help the student to take the next step: from compiling a reflective record to utilising that record as a tool to inform and to help to plan their personal professional development.

This development is important for all professionals in their continuing professional development. Its short-term importance becomes even more crucial for those students entering professions where their early professional competence and entry to membership of the professional body will be largely assessed through their written self-evaluation of their practical professional experience in employment.

▶ 7.3 Verbal communication skills

The development of fluent verbal communication skills is of value in a wide range of situations, from helping you to participate effectively in group seminar or tutorial sessions during your study, to preparing you for selection interviews when you come to apply for jobs, and to preparing you to explain briefs and proposals to clients in your future employment.

Students range from those with naturally shy and quiet personalities, who have to work hard in order to develop confidence in verbal communication, to those who have already actively participated in debate. Remember that, in common with other skills and competencies, verbal communication skills can be enhanced with practice and in response to constructive feedback. In this context, you should welcome opportunities to practise verbal communication in scenarios where you can receive constructive feedback, from which you can learn for the future.

The converse side of speaking skills is listening skills, as reflected in the old English proverb stating that 'silence is golden, speech is silver'. Effective communication skills comprise an ability to listen, as much as, if not more than, an ability to talk. You will only be effective as a team member if you listen to others in the team. In employment, you will only be effective in dealing with clients once you take the time and trouble to listen to them carefully in order to understand and interpret their requirements properly. You will only be effective in meetings and in debate if you listen and understand the viewpoints being proposed that are contrary to your own preferred point of view. Effective advocates are also effective listeners.

The importance of speaking and listening skills to the world of work means that these skills are often developed from an early point in your programme of study, often through the medium of an oral presentation to a group of students. The quality of an oral presentation will in part depend upon the quality of the material to be presented and therefore it is worthwhile to take the trouble to ensure that you have a clear and well argued statement to make. As in written communication, it is useful to open with a brief introduction to indicate the key points of your statement, and equally, to briefly summarise at the end for the benefit of the audience.

If you are asked to make an oral presentation, you are likely to be given an allocated time in which to do so. It is useful to rehearse your presentation by practising in front of a mirror and timing yourself, or preferably, by practising your presentation on a friend. Length and timing are important: so too is delivery. Observe teachers and academics in practice and think about the characteristics of teaching staff that make for a good speaker or a poor speaker. If you are provided with the opportunity to have your oral presentation videoed – take it! Watching the result will be of great benefit in helping you to identify the ways in which you move too much or too little; whether your eye contact with the audience is appropriate; and your audibility.

Don't be embarrassed about making mistakes, and take opportunities to learn and to enhance your verbal communication skills: you will reap the rewards when the time comes for challenging job interviews and crucial presentations to clients whom you are desperately keen to persuade to accept your viewpoint!

▶ 7.4 Visualisation and graphic communication skills

7.4.1 Visualisation
We see the built environment, and therefore skills and techniques connected with visualisation are an understandably important component of the students' repertoire. These skills may range from observation (that is, looking at buildings and observing them rather than merely seeing them), through visual display of material, to graphic visualisation using, for example, multimedia software.

Some of the related modules that you study may enhance skills that can assist you with the development of a more visual approach to the communication of ideas. For instance, the use of diagrammatic illustration in economics can help you to practise the expression of quite abstract concepts through drawing, as distinct from the written word. In studying management, diagrammatic representations can help you to understand different organisational structures and the resultant patterns and styles of decision making in organisations. In another context, diagrams can be used effectively to demonstrate the size and timing of income flows arising from specific financial investments.

Visual literacy is an important precursor to graphic communication skills. It is difficult to imagine someone being able to communicate their design concepts effectively without fluent visual literacy. People studying and working in the built environment need to be able to interpret drawings and plans; visualise the outcomes associated with the drawings or plans, and clearly communicate these outcomes to others.

The importance of visual skills in many aspects of Built Environment study and practice offers one reason why this area of professional study is comparatively attractive to students who find it difficult to communicate primarily through the medium of written explanation, such as those with dyslexia. Once the place of study provides appropriate understanding and support, dyslexic students can successfully complete degree courses in these fields. Indeed, my experience indicates that committed students can obtain good degrees.

7.4.2 Graphic communication skills

Graphic communication skills are relevant to a range of built-environment professionals who have to communicate the content and effects of plans and drawings to their clients. They are vital to the architects who create the drawings. In addition, surveyors and builders need to be able to communicate with clients and colleagues with respect to site drawings, while planners and urban designers need to communicate with respect to site and master plans.

Graphic communication skills are often an important complement to the verbal communication skills discussed above. At an early stage in your study, you may be asked to design and use fairly basic visual aids, such as simple overhead projection slides, to illustrate an oral presentation. Later, you should ensure that you develop more sophisticated graphic skills. To accompany oral presentations, you should master the use of a computer and appropriate software (such as Microsoft Powerpoint, at the time of writing). A well designed graphic presentation will greatly enhance your spoken words, not least because we use more of our brain to see than we do to listen.

For those studying construction, architecture and urban design, advanced computer-aided design skills will be essential and are discussed in section 7.7, about 'Information and communication technology skills'. It is perhaps axiomatic that planners must be able to read plans, that is, two-dimensional drawings of selected areas. However, buildings are three dimensional, and therefore architecture, construction, surveying and urban design students need to be able to read and to interpret three-dimensional drawings that demonstrate sections of a building or buildings, and also the different elevations of a building. Architects, at least, also need to be highly competent and skilled at drawing such three-dimensional drawings, preferably both freehand and also with the aid of a computer.

▶ 7.5 Team working

The Subject Benchmark Statement for Building and Surveying, written by the Quality Assurance Agency for Higher Education in the UK, states that graduates should be able to *'effectively work with others within the context of a team'* (QAA, 2002, 'Building and Surveying', p. 3). Built-environment professionals are likely to work in a variety of team situations. On occasion you will be working in a single-discipline, specialist, cognate team: for example, as one of a group of planners. On other occasions, you will work as a member of a multi-disciplinary team: for example, as a planner working alongside architects and civil engineers.

Because team working is an integral element of the working environment, most university courses ensure that there are opportunities to learn and to practise team-working skills during your course of study. These may be structured so that you are part of a single-discipline team exploring a cognate problem, or part of a multi-disciplinary team. Exercises in the latter category are often designed to encourage you to find out about the nature of related professions in the built environment.

For team-working exercises, you may be allocated into groups, or the formation of groups may be a matter of student choice. In the second case, where you have an input into the composition of your team, remember that successful teams are composed of individuals with diverse characteristics. A group of similar individuals working together will not achieve the breadth and diversity of thought attainable by a team composed of individuals with different skills and competencies.

Team and group working also provide an environment in which you will find it relatively easy to explore new ideas with your peers. Giving constructive criticism of the ideas of others and receiving constructive criticism of your own ideas is an important element in the refinement and improvement of those ideas. Again, peer-group criticism occurs in the real world of professional practice, and so, becoming accustomed to both giving and receiving criticism in a positive manner is an important element in the learning process for any future professional.

Where the teams with whom you work and study include representatives from built-environment professions other than your own specialism, you should gain knowledge of the roles and expertise expected of related professions in addition to knowledge of your own profession. In principle this experience should help to equip you for future employment and for working interprofessionally. However, in practice you should be thoughtful about the extent to which your programme of study equips you with the skills needed for interprofessional practice. Whyte and Edge (1999) argued that the design of many courses omits the content and methods necessary for the teaching of these skills, and there is little reason to believe that Built Environment courses in general are an exception.

Opportunities for team and group working should help you to improve your general ability to work effectively in teams and groups: a transferable skill that is valuable in many work situations. For example, when you sit down to prepare an individual assignment, you are primarily dependent upon your own time management, goal-setting and attainment skills in order to complete the assignment to your satisfaction and submit it on time. In contrast, when you work as part of a larger group – even a group of only two people – your ability to meet these goals becomes dependent upon the behaviour of other(s) as well as upon your own behaviour. Of course, this reflects the reality of employment: some tasks will be individual tasks but others will be group tasks. Opportunities to practise and develop the ability to understand group dynamics and to learn to work successfully with other people are therefore an important element of preparation for future employment.

The learning situation should enable you to analyse your own and others' relative strengths in a group environment and therefore prepare you to work more effectively in a group in future. You should reflect upon the following questions:

- How comfortable do I feel with different roles within a group?
- Do I prefer to organise activities or to focus upon doing those activities?
- Am I comfortable acting as group spokesperson?
- Do I find it easy or difficult to identify others' relative strengths and weaknesses and therefore to understand how best a particular team might operate effectively?

Teamwork is also about communication. To be successful, you must perform your assigned role to a high standard – and also communicate both progress and outcome clearly to the other members of the team. The person assigned to lead or chair the group must communicate so that everyone is clear as to their role and the framework within which it is to be carried out. The spokesperson will need to understand and be able to synthesise the results obtained by all the group members.

Teams do not always operate smoothly and so teamwork can provide opportunities for developing higher-order communication skills such as negotiation and dispute resolution. In Built Environment courses, group work will sometimes be designed to focus upon dispute resolution through role-play scenarios involving, for example, planners and real estate developers.

Teamwork and group work are essential life skills and therefore worth putting effort into. To illustrate this point, think about sports, especially team sports such as football, hockey or swimming. There may be individual star players but the whole team must work together effectively to ensure success. With a sport such as sailing, effective teamwork can be a matter of survival – so it is no surprise to find that experienced sailors nearly always excel in team situations.

A survey of built-environment employers and practitioners carried out by the Fund for the Development of Teaching and Learning (FDTL) Better Together research project (www.bettertogether.ac.uk 2001) found that a good understanding of teamwork was seen as a vital attribute of graduates in relation to their employability. This again reinforces the point that most individuals do not operate in isolation in their working environment.

▶ 7.6 Problem solving

At a basic level, all students will have developed some problem-solving skills during their education prior to embarking upon university study. For example, much of the standard mathematics repertoire consists of providing an accurate solution to set problems through the routine application of mathematical rules and formulae. Similar skills are important when studying introductory law or structural engineering.

As you progress through higher education, you will be expected to demonstrate higher-order problem-solving skills. For instance, many final-year programmes contain a summative integrative module, the assessment of which is based upon the student's capabilities in synthesising information, analysing a problem and suggesting a considered and appropriate solution. This approach requires a degree of independent thought far removed from the routine solution of standard problems found in basic mathematics. In the world of employment, problems are the rule rather than the exception. Therefore a good level of ability to think independently about practical problems and to propose practical solutions is an important skill in terms of the graduate's employability.

Students' problem-solving capabilities can be improved through problem-based learning techniques. These techniques are central to architectural education, where students expect to be presented with an outline design brief and to create their own solutions to the problems inherent in the brief that they have been given. In the other Built Environment disciplines the use of problem-based learning is, for the most part, more recent. One attraction of problem-based learning to both the educator and the student is that, in addition to enhancing the student's problem-solving skills, problem-based learning when used effectively also develops some of the other skills discussed in this chapter, in particular communication skills and team working. Where real-world problems are used, it can often also help students to investigate problems from an interdisciplinary, rather than a single-discipline, perspective.

Problem-based learning comes in many guises but will often involve a staged learning process:

- Introduction to the problem;
- inquiry and formation of hypothesis;
- independent research, including collection of data;
- testing of the hypothesis;
- evaluation and drawing of conclusions.

(Anderson, Louiscek and Webb, 2000).

To illustrate this process, we can draw upon the real-world example of a multiple retailer wishing to be advised by its real estate consultants as to whether or not to open a new store in a particular town centre. In a real estate programme, students will undertake this problem once they have completed their introductory studies and also received further teaching about the influences upon retail location.

- In stage 1, the lecturer provides the students with the problem outlined above. The students form teams of two or three in order to represent a real estate team. The task of each team is to advise the retailer with respect to a town centre location of their own choice.
- In stage 2, the students begin to ask questions and collect information. Each team is then in a position to develop hypotheses as to what characteristics would be required of a location in order for it to satisfy the need of the retailer.
- In stage 3, the students undertake some independent research, and collect some more refined data about the location that they are testing as a possible site for the retailer's new store. This will include primary research such as visits to the site, interviews with local real estate agents, or pedestrian flow counts.
- In stage 4, they can refine their data using relevant IT software, then each team can test the hypothesis as to whether their chosen location is suitable for the retailer or not.
- Stage 5 is the final stage, in which the data and their experience in tackling the problem are evaluated, allowing conclusions to be drawn as to the desirability of the site investigated for the retailer's new store.

Problem-based learning therefore takes students away from their textbooks and out of the lecture theatre, and encourages independent rather than dependent learning. Such an approach is known as 'active learning' and it will help the student to learn more effectively than will the passive learning attached to sitting in a classroom or solely reading books. One reason why problem-based learning is more common today than a decade ago is a simple one: information is now more ubiquitous. The internet means that more information is readily available at a computer, reducing the time taken to collate the initial information required for stage 2 of this approach. This availability of information then frees up more time for stages 3–5, allowing the students to develop their independent research and learning, then to share their results with the other members of the team in order to test and evaluate their hypothesis. The lecturer becomes the advisor throughout this process, with the students directing their own learning. So, remember that in order to gain the most benefit from problem-based learning, it is advisable to seek your lecturer's advice when appropriate, rather than to work solely on your own as a team of students!

▶ 7.7 Information and communication technology skills

Information and communication technology (ICT) skills are increasingly important in many aspects of everyday life, with both study and professional practice being no exception. At a minimum, word processing skills are useful to all students, while knowledge of spreadsheets is essential in surveying and real estate; and of computer-aided design in architecture, engineering and construction.

Students will be expected to be able to communicate with tutors and with fellow students through electronic mail. In addition, the internet is an increasingly important repository of materials to be accessed in order to study, and therefore an ability to use the web effectively is also an essential aspect of modern study.

At a more advanced stage in their studies, students use material retrieved from sources on websites and reference this material exactly as with material from the library. The precise specialist software skills that are needed will depend upon the particular subject of study within the built environment. In construction and architecture, expertise with computer-aided design packages will prove invaluable. For students of real estate, tailored valuation and property-management software will be more important.

Students also benefit from developing word processing skills: for a large-scale project report or for a written dissertation the ability to use the more advanced characteristics of a word processing package will prove of great assistance in the preparation, management and presentation of a large document. The ability to edit quickly leaves more time to improve upon the presentation of work, and good presentation helps to gain extra marks – at least it does if the content being presented is worthwhile!

► 7.8 Research skills

All students require reasonable research skills although they may not recognise that these are research skills (see also, Cottrell, 2003, chapter 6, for an introduction to this topic)! For example, students need to be able to take notes during lectures and other taught sessions in order to help them to learn the taught material. But note taking does not provide the key to successful study: the notes must be organised and filed so that they can be retrieved effectively when there is need to refer back to them. Summary note taking and the effective organisation of the notes are also essential research skills – ask anyone who has successfully completed a PhD thesis!

While most students are not academically inclined enough to attempt a PhD thesis, many postgraduate Masters programmes and some undergraduate degree programmes will require the successful completion of a dissertation. Such a dissertation requires you to master and to develop research skills. You will need to identify the problem to be researched, couched as a research hypothesis. You will need to think about *what* you are researching and, equally important, *why* your chosen dissertation topic matters. A review of recent literature about your chosen topic and related questions will help you to understand and refine your own research topic and its wider context.

Once you are confident that you know where your dissertation research is going, you must decide by what route you are going to reach your destination. This *how to* is your research methodology. You need to think about your chosen method of research and also what it can, and cannot, be expected to achieve. For an undergraduate dissertation, you will not be expected to have the sophisticated research methodology of a doctoral thesis, but equally, for a doctoral thesis you will require a more robust methodology than for an undergraduate dissertation.

Once you have applied your chosen methodology to undertake your primary research, you will have to analyse its results. This analysis will need to be carried out with a keen awareness of the reliability and reproduceability of your results. There is no point in conducting sophisticated statistical analysis on a limited range of subjective data. Again, the quantity and quality of data acceptable for an undergraduate dissertation will be less than that expected at postgraduate level.

Having analysed your results, you will need to synthesise them and consider their meaning in the context of the existing literature and your understanding of your research problem – problem-solving skills again! You must be aware both of the limitations of your own research and also of potential future research that could shed further light upon your core research topic.

If all of this sounds daunting, then remember that you should not, normally, be expected to undertake this type of research without support from an academic supervisor. Your supervisor is there to assist and will have far more research experience than you do – so make sure that you make use of it!

For the Built Environment subjects, recent UK Quality Assurance Agency Overview reports concerning the assessment of teaching quality in higher education for Planning, Land and Property Management and Building all praised the incorporation of research and consultancy into teaching. For example: 'examples of best practice use research . . . to inform curriculum innovation' (Quality Assurance Agency, *Building Overview*, 1998a), and 'research and analytical skills . . . in the best practice . . . explicitly structured within the curriculum' (Quality Assurance Agency, *Land and Property Management Overview*, 1998b).

A good academic department will seek to ensure that it enhances the links between teaching, research and professional practice, to the mutual benefit of pedagogy, research and professional practice, and so of its students.

At Oxford Brookes University, research undertaken into undergraduate students' perceptions of staff research found that students valued the positive spin-offs into teaching that derived from staff involvement in research. Students reported that research-active academics displayed both a good current knowledge of, and also enthusiasm for, their subject. The research activity of academic staff was also seen to add credibility both to the department and to the student's degree (Jenkins et al., 1998).

Further research at Brookes focusing upon the experience of taught postgraduate students has endorsed the importance of synergies between research and teaching. One important aspect of this more recent research is the implication for higher education of the growing number of taught postgraduate students who are either using postgraduate study to further their professional career development (outside an academic career) or self-funding – or both (Lindsay et al., 2002). These students value staff whose research is perceived as salient to the students' course content and hence the students' personal professional development – in other words, not necessarily pure research.

The style and content of both teaching and research vary across disciplines from, for example, science to the humanities. Because many of the Built Environment subject disciplines, in common with some social sciences such as Geography, encompass a wide range of subject methodologies, students will find a range of teaching–research approaches and links even within cognate courses.

The strength of the links between research and research skills and teaching depend upon the strength of the research culture within the department and the course. The contribution of active researchers to the teaching programme; informal seminars; and accessible summaries of current research through the distribution of internal newsletters; all help to create and to rein-force the research ethos of the students' study environment. This link is perhaps clearest where staff research interests directly inform the curricu-lum content, with topics being informed by current staff research topics as distinct from alternative criteria.

While a research ethos should be stronger within postgraduate than undergraduate programmes, for undergraduate programmes too, students can develop and benefit from research skills. This is frequently reflected in the requirement for a dissertation or extended essay within the summative modules of an undergraduate programme. However, research skills can be developed in other interesting ways. Research skills can be encouraged through diverse means, ranging from a review of a selected part of the salient literature; to devising a project outline or a response to a project brief; to analysing real data; to using peer review within seminars; to presenting results. Peer-review skills are linked to skills of judgement and communication.

Some of these diverse research skills can be recognised as information-management skills. Today such information-management skills are a vital tool to aid the professional. This is partly due to the speed of change of infor-mation that soon loses it's currency. It is also because of the sheer scale of the contemporary information base. Today, this information base is too broad to be wholly covered by any single university programme of study. Instead, universities specialise in order to offer courses that make the most of the particular teaching and research expertise of their staff.

So graduates should leave university with the research and information-management skills that will equip them to navigate effectively through large amounts of information in order to select what is relevant, question it, and act upon it.

Finally, awareness that today's students are embarking upon a path of life-long learning means that all undergraduate, and much taught postgraduate, education is no longer the end of the educational process. The recognition that students need to be prepared for a life of learning is reflected in learn-ing outcomes designed to ensure that graduates are equipped as indepen-dent learners. This in itself raises the profile of research skills and processes within higher education.

▶ 7.9 Written competencies

7.9.1 Professional and academic writing
The written competencies that young students embarking upon an under-graduate programme of study straight after school need to develop should

lead them away from an essay format towards the structure and style of professional report used in the workplace. For built-environment professionals, the ability to author, analyse and critique written reports is an essential element of their working life. The transition process can be painful – report writing is far more concise and succinct than the usual essay style. It is therefore important for the student to be aware of what is required. Should paragraphs be numbered? Should bullet points be used? How should sources by referenced?

In contrast, a mature student returning to study after a period in employment may find it equally difficult to adjust to the requirements of academia. In the workplace, brevity and conciseness are to be applauded – in contrast, academics are often seeking a clearer step-by-step approach to the explanation of an argument by their students. This is one of the key means by which the tutor can verify that the student has understood the study material, as distinct from memorising the textbook.

Written work on the built environment can often be enriched through the use of questions that require the student to apply theoretical concepts to a real-life case study. The ability to apply theory to practice is also a good test of the student's understanding as well as being a useful part of the preparation for future employment.

For many courses, written competencies are also tested to the full in the final semester in the form of an extended essay or dissertation upon a specialist topic. This enables the students to investigate a topic of their choice on depth and should therefore be intellectually rewarding and stimulating. For those students to whom the written word does not come naturally, however, the physical task of writing such a lengthy written piece of work can prove physically and mentally demanding. Again, this is an aspect of alternative courses that you should consider in making your initial choice of course.

Whether the written piece of work is long or short, discursive or concise in style, do not forget the basic skills expected in your writing as a student. Always clearly reference source material – and always use the spell-check to check word processed documents. Bad spelling does not convey a professional impression to either an academic tutor or an employer!

7.9.2 Writing skills

So, in more detail, what are the specific writing skills to which you should pay attention during your degree programme? Some you may have met before in other contexts, but some may serve to distinguish writing about the built environment from, say, the arts or humanities. With regard to the built environment, you are likely to be asked to develop the ability to reason logically; to present a written critical analysis of research and/or commercial data; and to link the world of theory to that of professional practice.

Readers will find full coverage of the study skills required for academic writing in the specialist study skills books such as Cottrell (2003), chapters 7, 8, and 9. Here, the most important writing skills are summarised as the abilities to:

- Answer the question posed – in other words, to write a relevant response! This should be done in such a way as to answer the question in the manner intended by the questioner. For example, as you progress through a programme of study, you should find that questions asking you to *describe* or *explain* are increasingly replaced by questions asking you to *analyse*, to *critically assess* or to *evaluate*. Solely descriptive material will not be adequate to attain a pass standard after your initial study of a new subject!

- Distinguish between the more important and the less important; the more relevant and the less relevant information with respect to the question that you are investigating. This is particularly important when you are working within a tight word limit – itself a test of your ability to express yourself concisely and to summarise sometimes complex information effectively.

- Construct a logical argument or series of ideas compiled in a logical progression so that your written work is well structured and the direction of your thoughts is clear to the reader.

- Utilise and analyse the relevant theoretical concepts and frameworks in structuring your answer, remembering to explain the key concepts to the reader and to demonstrate your awareness of their limitations.

- Make appropriate use of empirical evidence and practical examples to illustrate your argument and to help you to give a critical account of the usefulness of the related theory that you are considering. In the built environment, the relationship between practicality and theory is an important one – and the importance of this relationship should be echoed in your writing.

At an advanced level of study, writing should reflect the ability to make a critical evaluation of the arguments and evidence. The line of argument, analysis and commentary should be clear, with appropriate referencing to the source materials.

▶ 7.10 Numeracy

Within the built environment, numeracy is particularly important to those working within the realms of construction, real estate and surveying. Architects and planners need to understand costs and the implications of costs, while builders and surveyors need to be able not only to understand but also to generate and to manipulate numerical data. For example, building surveyors must be able to calculate the load-bearing properties of structures; quantity surveyors to estimate costs and quantities; and real estate professionals to calculate property valuations.

At an introductory level, students may be asked to present numerical data and numerical relationships in graphs, tables or pie charts within modules in economics or surveying. Because the built environment is about buildings, it is important to be able to understand and to calculate spatial concepts such as area.

If you have not studied mathematics recently before embarking upon your study of the built environment, you can expect to have to revise your knowledge of the calculation of averages and percentages. But, if you are not confident with mathematics, be assured that the level of the mathematical technique that you will normally need in order to be able to manipulate numbers for yourself will not be very advanced. Computers and spreadsheet software take a lot of the hard work out of modern number crunching – but you will need to understand the basic concepts and the rationale for the numerical manipulations or you will not be able to use the software tools effectively or accurately.

At a more advanced level of your programme of study, you will be required to interpret and to manipulate data, possibly using appropriate statistical techniques of analysis such as regression. You will almost certainly be expected to be able to read statistical data and to understand its usefulness and its limitations.

Students of real estate will need slightly different mathematical techniques because the entire premise of real estate valuation is based upon the estimation of today's value in light of the future timestream of revenue and costs associated with the property to be valued. For this reason, methods for estimating rates of return over a period of time, such as discounted cash flow, are central to the analysis of real estate valuations. For the non-mathematician, much of the necessary mathematics is often embedded within contemporary computer software, which considerably simplifies the mathematical skill required by the valuer today.

▶ 7.11 Management and leadership

Managers can facilitate the attainment of objectives or they can create barriers to their attainment. One particular problem faced by the built environment in the opening decade of the twenty-first century appears to be the reluctance of a proportion of the older generation of managers and professionals to change and adapt. The notion that, because 'we've always done it this way', this is the best way, has inhibited the progress of professional practice in the built environment.

Proactive management is also about leadership and about having vision. For example, in the context of the urban environment, vision is required in order to ensure that a holistic approach is taken to its management and development. Without the unifying view provided by effective leadership, changes effected upon the built environment would be piecemeal and disjointed, lacking harmony of design or purpose.

It is regrettable that on occasion, and perhaps particularly in the public sector, management structures and financial constraints have made it difficult to work towards a unified vision for the future, to the detriment of the built environment.

Management and leadership are also worth acquiring and improving in their own right, because they are transferable in the workplace. They will stand you in good stead whatever your future career path. Effective management also helps to achieve an interdisciplinary approach to solving the multi-faceted problems that characterise the built environment.

Meanwhile, how can you expect to be able to develop management and leadership during your programme of study?

To start with, many students find that their personal time management is quite a challenge, especially in the diverse and diverting environment of university. So, one key skill for all students to learn at an early stage is that of personal time management. How do you ensure that you do actually do a full week's study in view of all the potential distractions associated with the active sports and social facilities available on campus? The establishment of a routine that suits you and enables you to attain a full week's work must be a priority. This is particularly true where courses contain few lectures and seminars but quite a lot of time for individual study. In addition to time, you will need to manage your use of the resources available to support your study. These resources range from subject and module student guides, to the relevant books and journals in the library, and relevant resources available electronically.

In order to study successfully, you will have to refine your time-management skills. Assessed coursework and preparation for examinations require students to work to a deadline and to organise their time in order to meet that deadline effectively. At the introductory level, the assessment tasks and so the self-organisation of time needed in order to complete these tasks will be comparatively straightforward. Towards the culmination of your studies, more complex assessment tasks, such as the preparation and submission of a large project or of a dissertation, will require more sophisticated organisation and time management. Now your time-management skills are evolving into the project-management skills that are an essential element of all management in the workplace and certainly important to management situations in the built environment!

The completion of a complex individual task such as a dissertation, or individual project, requires you to have developed your abilities as an independent learner. This capacity to project-manage your individual learning will prepare you well for working without constant supervision once you are in employment. No-one wants to spend all their time telling the new graduate employee exactly what to do all the time!

In addition, your abilities as an independent learner will also equip you well to develop as a career professional in the built environment. The professional bodies normally require their members to undertake a minimum amount of Continuing Professional Development (CPD) every year. While some of this CPD may be attained through attendance at relevant courses, some of it is likely to depend upon your own private study. One objective of higher education Built Environment programmes is therefore to equip you to carry on with your lifelong learning after you have left formal study.

So far, we have primarily looked at management and leadership through the perspective of the individual. However, in practice you cannot perform as an effective manager or leader in isolation. Effective management and leadership depend upon the effective use of some team-working skills – and upon effective communication skills both as a speaker and as a listener. Group seminar and group assessment activities provide valuable opportunities for you to develop the skills necessary for working with others. These skills are also necessary for managing other people. You need to develop a keen awareness of both your role and your responsibilities and also the role and responsibilities of the other members of the team. Leadership is about motivating your team members to complete the task to time and to standard – preferably above the expected standard.

Practice at teamwork should also provide you with opportunities to organise meetings and to participate effectively in meetings. Remember that you must have a clear objective for your meeting – and that a successful meeting is one that reaches its objective within a reasonable timescale, having allowed those participating to express and consider their own and others' viewpoints.

A good course of study will prepare you for the world of work – but you need to be aware of how this is happening and to articulate this to potential employers when you are applying for jobs.

▶ 7.12 Inter- and multi-disciplinarity

Interdisciplinarity exists where there is a clear cross-fertilisation between two or more subjects, resulting in a weakening of the dividing boundary between them. Because of the breaking down of barriers involved, interdisciplinary study can be more challenging than the study of a single, clearly demarcated subject. For this reason, while interdisciplinarity can be enriching to the study experience, it is a skill that needs to be learned and therefore needs to be taught. Oxley and Glover (2002, p. 7) point to the following as general principles to be followed if interprofessional education is to be effective, and analogous principles are to apply more widely to effective interdisciplinary learning:

*   learning objectives that are both clear to, and valued by, all participants;
*   curriculum design that is flexible enough to accommodate both generic content relevant to all participant professions and also single-discipline-specific content;
*   curriculum design that explicitly incorporates the dynamics and boundaries of the different disciplines and professions;
*   programmes that provide interdisciplinary learning opportunities at times throughout the programme of study, and accord this a status equal to that of discipline-specific content and skills through the assessment strategy;
*   provision for feedback to, and reflection by, students upon the interdisciplinary elements of their programme.

Some learning skills are more discipline-specific than others. In this respect, some skills strengthen multi disciplinarity, within which divisions between the different bodies of knowledge and professional skills are retained and valued. Such clear individual subject identity is a welcome counterpart to a strongly identifiable professional culture embodied in the role of the professional institution.

Some skills are more transferable across individual subjects and so contribute to an interdisciplinary and potentially interprofessional approach to the built environment. A different perspective is offered where skill development is linked to underlying issues such as the environment, development or sustainability. For example, it could be argued that interprofessionality in the built environment is a necessary condition for the attainment of environmental sustainability.

An effective course of study can yield a rich matrix of skills within which the discipline-specific is interwoven with the interdisciplinary. This is a real potential strength of courses for the built environment professions and for their development, once a balance between the individual culture of the different constituent subjects and an understanding of their wider interdisciplinary context is attained and enriched.

8 Learning and assessment

Having looked at studying and skills needed for a career in the built environment, this chapter now deals with the assessment that follows. In addition to the traditional examination, the very wide range of coursework methods of assessment are explained.

Architecture students at Oxford Brookes value opportunities for the visual and verbal presentation of their work as a means of assessment, and see little value in unseen examinations. On the other hand, real estate management students have indicated that a range of assessment methods are valuable, reflecting the characteristic diversity of their programme of study.

New students were asked to comment upon the perceived usefulness of the different methods of assessment that they would experience during their university study, and their responses are summarised in Table 8.1. The responses from new real estate management students highlighted the perceived importance of writing professional reports and providing visual presentations as modes of assessment. Incoming architecture students identified opportunities for the visual and verbal presentation of their work as particularly important and, like the continuing architecture students, saw limited value in examinations as a mode of assessment.

Table 8.1 illustrates the variety of assessment, and stresses the fact that the traditional unseen examination is by no means considered by the students to be either the main or the most appropriate mode of assessment for Built Environment courses.

This diversity of types of assessment means that academics have to take care to ensure that a student's programme of study contains an appropriate mix of assessments. Courses therefore have an associated strategy that seeks to ensure that there is a sensible balance and mix of assessment activities during the student's learning. A good strategy should ensure that assessment helps the students to learn and therefore supports their educational development through the course.

Table 8.1 Assessment – the student perspective

Assessment method	Architecture	Real Estate Management
Visual presentation	83%	52%
Verbal presentation	59%	48%
Report writing	56%	60%
Examinations	22%	33%

▶ 8.1 Assessment

8.1.1 Diagnostic, formative and summative assessment

As well as the variety of types of assessment, which are discussed individually later in this chapter, assessment may be diagnostic, formative or summative.

Diagnostic assessment is designed to help students to test their comprehension of the study material so as to recognise weaknesses and difficulties at an early stage in order that these may be addressed and rectified. Diagnostic assessment in the first term of a programme of study can help to assess the ease or difficulty with which the student is coping with skills and subject matter that are different from his or her previous learning experience. This is especially important in those Built Environment subjects that do not directly follow on from subjects traditionally taught in secondary education. For example, architecture students benefit from diagnostic testing of their architectural drawing skills at an early stage, and real estate management students benefit from diagnostic testing of their numeracy.

Formative assessment is assessment that is not formally marked, so that it does not contribute to the student's formal result at the end of the module or unit of study. Formative assessment is designed to provide students with feedback during their study and so to inform them as to their progress, and their strengths and weaknesses with respect to their studies. Timely formative assessment results will be returned to the student in good time to allow for response and improvement prior to the summative assessment of the module. Many students enter a programme of study with a fairly instrumental approach and ignore formative assessment because it does not directly contribute to the final mark. This is a mistake: make use of the opportunities provided by formative assessment to find out how you are progressing and to correct weaknesses before you submit summative assessments.

As should be clear from the above context, summative assessments are those assessments designed to capture the sum of the student's learning at a particular point during the programme of study. The criteria for the assessment will be designed so as to test the extent to which the student has achieved the learning outcomes associated with the module being studied. At a more advanced stage of study, assessment may be synoptic across more than one module in order to encourage synthesis and a drawing together of the separate components of study into the multi-disciplinary approach that fits more closely into the real world of professional practice in the built environment.

8.1.2 Assessment criteria

As noted above, assessment criteria are designed so as to test the extent to which the student has achieved the learning outcomes of the module – or modules – of study. At introductory stages of a subject, individual modules are normally assessed separately. However, as the student progresses to more advanced study, it is more likely that assessment will also test his or her ability to draw together the learning outcomes from more than one module. This is most often achieved through project or design work: a project may require a construction management student to consider both the management, legal, and health and safety aspects of a construction project; a design project may require an architecture student to consider both the creative visual design and also the construction technology associated with a building or group of buildings.

Clearly stated assessment criteria are important to the student: after all, you will want to know what the tutor is looking for before you devote time to the aspect to be assessed. Coursework and project work will often make the assessment criteria clear, but if this is not the case, do not be afraid to ask.

Assessment criteria will take the form of asking you to ensure that the coursework submitted for assessment achieves some of the following types of objectives:

- clarity of methodology and/or structure of argument;
- analysis of data and/or theory;
- the application of theory to practice;
- clear introduction, conclusions and recommendations;
- style and presentation of submitted material.

Coursework will then by assessed according to the extent to which the criteria are achieved and the quality of that achievement. Sometimes individual assessment criteria are explicitly weighted with different percentages of the total marks. This is likely to indicate that the marks available for the quality of presentation are less than those available for the quality of analysis. For project work and/or for more advanced work, it is less likely that individual components will be assigned individual marks: in these cases, the assessor will be marking against the criteria in light of the overall performance of the submitted work in order to allow for the synergies between the separate categories, associated with a more synoptic approach to assessment at a more advanced level.

▶ 8.2 Assessment by examination

Examinations remain a common form of summative assessment, in particular with respect to those degree courses that are linked to professional accreditation. For this reason, the following section of this chapter offers some help concerning both your examination preparation and your examination technique. If you are worried by the prospect of examination papers, this should prove useful, especially if combined with other sources of advice such as Cottrell (2003), chapter 12. If you have already undertaken a number of examinations and feel more confident with your examination approach and technique, read on: there are pointers below to help you to reflect upon your current approach and to improve upon it for the future.

8.2.1 Preparing for revision

You need to establish some priorities for revision
Your revision should cover the full spread of your course or module: students are often tempted to begin their revision at the beginning of their notes and to work in detail so that they never reach the end before the examination date! This lack of strategy precludes them from attempting to answer any questions based upon the later sections of their studies. Your revision may be selective rather than comprehensive but ensure that you retain enough breadth of coverage to reflect the course content sensibly in your examination script, and do not limit yourself to the first half only!

Revision that emphasises the early part of a course can also be a dangerous approach in that it results in an examination script lacking in depth. The early parts of a course are normally easier than the later parts: if your examination answers cannot demonstrate understanding at the level of the final learning outcomes of the course, you cannot expect to perform well in the examination assessment.

Revision should be exactly that: a revisiting of, and reflection upon, the material that you have studied. Revision should be an active process, encouraging you to engage again with the course material and so to deepen your understanding of it. The examiner will be looking for evidence of understanding in addition to a knowledge of basic principles: pure memory and rote learning of facts in isolation will not score high marks in degree-level examinations. As study of this book should be demonstrating, built-environment professionals need to be able to understand and to apply their knowledge to real-world situations, and examinations often reflect this underlying philosophy.

As part of your preparation for your revision, reflect upon your recent study and identify those parts of the course where you particularly want to improve your understanding. Make use of section headings, lecture titles and the headings of key chapters in textbooks to help you to structure your revision.

Revision notes structured with the help of section headings and subheadings will help you prepare to write good examination answers. Each paragraph in your answer should deal with one key point, or the material covered by a heading. If the opening sentence of each paragraph incorporates key words or a key phrase from your revision, this will help to give you confidence that your writing is a reflection of your revision as you write during the pressure of examination. Your paragraph can then follow through with the material that you have revised in relation to that key word or key phrase, in order to amplify it, either through a more discursive explanation or by the use of one or two illustrative examples to demonstrate your understanding of the headlined material.

You can incorporate diagrams and charts into your revision to create pictures in your mind. This strategy will help you to remember facts more easily, as you may find it easier to visualise a picture than a piece of written text or even a list of bullet points.

Practising relevant diagrams as an integral part of your revision will also help you to utilise diagrams constructively in your examination answers. Practice will improve your diagrams if not make them perfect! If you do not feel confident with diagrams, begin with a simple version and slowly build upon this foundation. For example, in an economics module you could start with a simple 'supply and demand' diagram. A next step would be to draw – and be careful to distinguish between – shifts of, and movements along, the demand and supply curves. Once you feel more confident, you could incorporate different demand and supply elasticities. A similar step-by-step approach will help you to revise and develop diagrams with which to illustrate your answers effectively in other subjects.

Beginning to revise for an examination can be daunting, especially if you have not found the module easy to study. Start with a topic that you enjoyed and spent a reasonable amount of time studying. You should then be able to get into a smooth pace for your revision and, hopefully, enjoy revisiting and enhancing your knowledge of the module.

8.2.2 How to answer examination questions

Use past examination questions

Make a positive effort to obtain and to study previous examination papers and/or sample examination papers and questions during your revision. These should help provide guidance as to both the type and the range of questions that you can expect to find on your examination paper. Ask your tutor if you can expect any particular difference in the number or style of questions compared with past papers. This guidance will help you to think in advance of your own examination about the type of questions that you prefer to answer and those questions about which you might feel less confident. Once you are well established in your revision, try out some previous questions and see how difficult or easy you find it to attempt to answer them. This exercise will help you to clarify your ideas about which of the questions you would like to answer on your examination paper.

Once you are realistic and do not expect to write a perfect answer to a question when you are only half way through your revision, practising preparing examination answers will be very useful. The more closely you can discipline yourself to simulate examination conditions while you attempt practice questions, for example by ensuring that you have some uninterrupted time in a quiet room, the more realistic and useful the exercise will be.

Structure your answers

How you structure your answer is important and will affect the final mark that you achieve. The following general guidelines will therefore help you:

- Keep your introduction brief. Your introduction may interpret the question in your own words or state what the question is about, and outline how you intend to answer it. Avoid unduly lengthy introductions as these will take time and space away from the core of your answer.
- Define any key terms or underlying assumptions that are central to your answer.
- Explain the relevant theory or context to your answer, including a brief explanation of the basic ideas and/or rationale.
- Remember to make use of diagrams and/or calculations where relevant. In subjects such as building or economics, a diagram will help you to convey ideas quickly so that you can provide a fuller answer within the time constraints of the examination. In valuations, annotated calculations and appropriate diagrams mean that your answer may contain just enough written text to emphasise key points for the examiner. For drawings, diagrams and calculations, remember to keep them simple, logical and labelled for maximum clarity.

- Develop your argument. You should demonstrate your reasoning by propounding a balanced point of view based upon discussion of the relative merits of both sides of an argument. One particular aspect of this approach is sometimes used in law examinations. The question may provide a scenario with respect to a client, and your answer will take the form of a balanced consideration of the arguments underlying the postulated scenario, followed by a summary of your advice to the client.
- Be critical but constructive. Reinforce your points with supporting facts and/or practical examples whenever possible. Be rational and objective: you are writing an examination answer and not an article for a tabloid newspaper!
- One principle of journalism, however, can be of help to you. As indicated in the previous section, ensure that the first sentence of your paragraph contains the key message to be covered in that paragraph, just as the opening sentence(s) of a newspaper article convey the key message to be covered by that article. Then use the remaining sentences of the paragraph to amplify and to exemplify your main point.
- Finish your answer with a brief summary conclusion that relates the argument propounded in your answer back to the examination question.

Be relevant!
One crucial piece of guidance on answering examination questions is: Be relevant! Answer the question that has been set on the examination paper and not a different question that you had hoped to see on the paper!

8.2.3 In the examination
In the examination:

- Keep calm and have belief in yourself: if you have prepared sensibly for the examination, you will be able to do yourself justice in answering the questions.
- Read the examination paper carefully, including the instructions – the rubric – at the heading of the paper. Do attempt all of the questions that you need to answer.
- Choose carefully the questions that you wish to answer, then check the instructions again to ensure that you have chosen the correct number and combination of questions. For example, if an examination paper is set in two parts, Part A and Part B, you may be required to answer three questions including at least one from each of Part A and Part B, leaving you a free choice for your third question.
- Think about what the instruction contained within the question is asking you to do and ensure that, in answering the question, you will obey the

instruction. For example, you may be asked to *analyse*, which means to break down a complex statement into its component parts; to *consider*, that is, to weigh up merits after careful thought; to *discuss*, which is to examine through written argument; or to *evaluate*, that is, to assess the statement contained in the examination question.

- Think about the main points that you wish to make for each answer before you begin to write your answer. Whether or not you prefer to write an outline before writing your full answer is entirely up to you. Many students like to jot down a brief list of their key points to ensure that they do not omit any vital points in the stress of the examination. But you must avoid writing lengthy plans for your answer that leave you insufficient time to write your formal answer.

- Spend sensible amounts of time on each question, allocating your time in proportion to the marks available. For example, if a compulsory question on the examination paper carries half of the total marks available, then you should spend about half of the time available in the examination upon that question.

- Re-read the question while writing your answer, to ensure that your answer remains relevant and clearly directed towards answering that question.

- Ensure that essay-style answers have a brief introduction and conclusion, with a discussion of the key points in between.

- Ensure that calculation-based answers clearly explain your method and annotations: mathematical accuracy is not the only skill being tested by the examiners.

- Illustrate theory and ideas with practical examples when possible, to demonstrate that you understand the relevance and application of the theory.

- Leave yourself a few minutes to read and check your answers.

- Write legibly and present your answers neatly.

- It should not happen, but if you do find that you are running out of time during an examination try not to panic. Write or draw an outline of what you would have submitted in detail given more time – this is more effective than leaving your answer half finished.

8.2.4 Different examination formats

Unseen examinations

On many Built Environment courses, especially those undergraduate courses carrying professional accreditation, traditional examinations are widely used as a mode of assessment. In this context, traditional examinations are those where the students do not see the examination paper until after they have entered the examination room, and then write their answers under controlled conditions, submitting these answers for assessment before leaving the room. Traditional examinations have the benefits of testing students' learning over a range of the module learning outcomes, and ensuring that it is the student who writes the answers. In addition, it can be argued that the pressure of the traditional unseen examination exposes students to the pressures of the professional workplace and tests their ability to cope with those pressures.

There are three main disadvantages of unseen examinations as a means of assessment. First, they encourage students to memorise quantities of course content, rather than reflecting upon that content and achieving a deeper understanding. Secondly, as unseen examination papers often contain an element of student choice regarding which questions to answer, they encourage students to learn selectively, rather than learning all parts of the module. Thirdly, students are subject to high levels of pre-examination stress and so their performance in the examination may not always reflect their underlying competence under more normal conditions.

In response to these limitations of the unseen examination as a means of assessment, a number of variants have evolved and these are described below.

Open-book examinations

Where a module being examined relies heavily upon a single text for reference, allowing students to bring their copy of the text into the examination can shift the emphasis of the examination from memorising facts to understanding the module's components. One example is law, where students may be allowed to bring a text citing case law into the examination. The student who has studied conscientiously during the module will be familiar with the book and therefore be able to use it rapidly as a reference text to supplement the examination answers. The student who has been less conscientious will find it much more difficult to make effective use of the text under the time constraints of examination conditions.

Revealed examination papers

There are various ways of using this examination technique but the broad principles are the same. At the beginning of the module, the tutor provides all students with the examination paper for the module. As an example, this may consist of eight questions, one for each of the eight topics covered by the module. The tutor advises the students that their final examination will comprise three questions from the menu of eight topics. There will be no choice – the students will be expected to answer all three of the chosen questions.

One benefit of this examination technique is that students are motivated to study the entire course rather than being selective, as may be the case where examination papers offer a choice. A further benefit is that pre-examination stress is decreased because students can prepare themselves for the actual questions to be asked. The technique also assists those students who have mastered the module well to achieve better examination results. Experience suggests that this examination technique does enhance the marks achieved at the top end of the mark range. On the other hand, the examination answers are no longer being prepared wholly under controlled conditions, and so students may be seeking external help in the preparation of their answers.

Take-away examination papers
In this case, instead of students entering a room to sit an examination paper, students take the examination paper away and submit their answers at the end of a specified period of time, such as four days. So, for example, the examination paper might be made available at 09.00 on Monday morning and students required to submit their answer papers by 16.00 on Thursday afternoon.

Take-away examination papers therefore become a hybrid between the traditional examination and coursework. The ability to memorise material and to write it down quickly is less important than with the traditional unseen examination. Instead, it is the ability to find and use appropriate resources and to draft polished answers within a given timescale that becomes important. Take-away examination papers can be more appropriate than traditional examination papers in some circumstances, especially in postgraduate courses. This is because they provide the facility to test deeper learning rather than the memorisation of knowledge.

One limitation of this examination technique is that students may be subject to stress during the answer period. In addition, as with all coursework, there is less check that students are providing their own unassisted work than is the case in the traditional examination.

Oral examinations
Oral examinations are one means of assessing the oral communication skills described in Chapter 7. In this respect, they also provide some useful practice for the face-to-face interview that often forms part of the recruitment and selection process when graduates are applying for jobs. When oral examinations are used to test the attainment of oral communication skills, the whole student cohort will be subject to the same assessment.

In contrast, oral examinations may also be used to assess a small proportion of students. Where there is doubt as to whether to award a student a mark above or below a defined mark boundary, an oral examination may be used as an additional discriminator in order to arrive at the final mark. In a more negative context, an oral examination is also a useful means of checking the authenticity of the work submitted by a student on those occasions when this is in reasonable doubt.

Oral examinations can provide an opportunity for students to offer more flexible answers than they can do in a written examination. They also require students to respond quickly and to be able to defend their own arguments, as they will need to do in professional situations.

Oral examinations require specialist interviewing skills on the part of those conducting the examination, including the abilities to focus upon the objective assessment criteria and to ignore subjectivity, which also apply to other means of assessment. As with a written examination, all students will be asked the same questions, and questions will be structured so that they elicit a hierarchy of responses, from the relatively easy to the difficult, in order that the marks awarded can discriminate accurately between the poor and good responses.

If you are to take an oral examination, take time to prepare for it adequately. Where students do not have a basic knowledge of the subject, this inadequacy can show through quickly in an oral examination. In contrast, where students have genuinely mastered a topic, an oral examination provides a flexible framework within which they can explore the subject in depth and communicate their understanding and enthusiasm in order to gain high marks.

Good luck with your revision and the examinations that are an inevitable component of assessment for most courses. I hope that this section will have helped you to think positively, and no doubt you will have other ideas of your own to help you prepare for your course examinations.

▶ 8.3 Coursework

8.3.1 Coursework – general guidance

'Coursework' is the generic term applied to work that is subject to formal assessment in other forms than that of an examination. In recent decades, the diversity of assessment has widened considerably. There are a number of reasons for this growing diversity, not least the recognition that, while examinations are an effective method for testing competencies such as the ability to analyse ideas through written communication, students learn other competencies and skills during their programme of study and many of these are more effectively tested in other ways.

This introductory section therefore offers some guidance with respect to coursework of fairly general applicability. The following sections outline the main characteristics of different coursework forms, while a later section considers the nature of dissertations in more detail because these form a major component of assessment for many courses, especially postgraduate courses.

For all coursework, it is important to read carefully through the question or brief provided by the tutor. Is what is expected from you in preparing the assessment clear to you? For example:

- Is there a single component to the coursework such as writing an essay? Or are there multiple components such as making a presentation and writing a report?
- Are the assessment criteria clearly stated?
- Is this coursework to be undertaken on an individual basis or as part of a group of students?

If you have questions, ensure that you contact the tutor and seek clarification. Where there are additional opportunities to discuss the progress of your coursework, take advantage of these opportunities for guidance. Such opportunities will not always be provided, because sometimes the ability to resolve a problem independently is one of the competencies being tested.

Coursework often provides a good medium for the testing of the skills, in addition to the knowledge, learnt during a module of study. For example, the format may require demonstration of IT skills with respect to word processing or spreadsheets; or presentation elements may require visual, IT or verbal communication skills. In some cases, coursework may be wholly computer based. Multiple-choice questions may be available as a diagnostic assessment to enable you and your tutor to check your progress with understanding basic course concepts, and computer-based assignments may also be used for summative assessment to be submitted electronically to the tutor.

8.3.2 Short-answer and multiple-choice exercises

Items of assessment are not all lengthy and are not all summative. Useful formative assessment can be the result of students' completing short-answer exercises. These can either be in the form of quizzes or quick tests, or may take the form of drafting an outline plan for an exam or essay question. Short-answer questions are useful for helping students to check their understanding of the material studied. As they are not summative, they can be used during small-group teaching situations with students marking their own or each other's answers. Short-answer exercises have the advantage of requiring students to supply their own answers (in contrast to multiple-choice questions, where a range of possible answers are supplied).

Multiple-choice exercises consist of a question or an incomplete statement followed by four or five suggested answers or ways of completing the statement, of which most responses will be incorrect, with one response being the correct answer. At their simplest, such exercises help students to check their knowledge of basic concepts and technical vocabulary, enabling the student to clear up misunderstandings at an early stage. Straightforward multiple-choice questions with an immediate scoring system are an ideal vehicle for allowing students to work independently and to learn and remember concepts and formulae. Learning the technical vocabulary of a new subject can be analogous to learning a foreign language and so similar self-testing exercises can assist with students' knowledge retention.

Multiple-choice questions can also be designed to be more complex in order to develop students' problem-solving skills. Rather than the single-step question described above, a logical sequence of simple steps will lead to the correct answer. At each point, the student will need to answer a question correctly in order to pass on to the next step, and if they provide an inaccurate answer, a written explanation of that step will be available to help their understanding.

This type of exercise can be assessed relatively easily, thus providing an effective mechanism for diagnostic or formative assessment. Summative assessments may also be designed for completion under controlled conditions, either on paper or at the computer, and submitted electronically for marking. When more complex exercises have to be undertaken online, then naturally the students' IT skills are being tested at the same time as their knowledge of the programme content!

8.3.3 Written assessment: essays and reports

Essays have the advantage of allowing the student an element of choice as to the exact argument and content of their answer. A typical essay question will invite the student to *discuss*, *explain* or *examine* a viewpoint or a statement. At a more advanced level, these terms are often replaced by verbs such as *assess*, *analyse* or *evaluate*. The nature of the essay question and the context of the module and its indicative reading will often make the direction of the required answer clear, but, if this is not the case, do not hesitate to ask the tutor for clarification rather than risk spending time upon a potentially misdirected answer.

One objective of studying the built environment is preparation for professional practice and so essays may be used to encourage an element of role play. A role-play question helps to place theoretical principles in the practical context of their application. For example, an essay may take the form of providing advice to the managing director of a company as to the feasibility of a proposed property development project.

When the tutor wishes to assess students' understanding of specific ideas or techniques, the essay question may be longer and structured so as to highlight parts of the content that must be covered in the essay. For example, a real estate student may be asked to explain two named valuation techniques and then discuss their relative merits.

Essay titles may also contain numerical data in order to test students' ability to analyse and interpret data in relation to principles that have been learnt. This can be quite testing for those students who have relied on memory alone in their study rather than thinking through and understanding the material. For example, an economics question might contain a set of data relating to changes in interest rates and household income and then ask the student to apply this information to the housing market.

In summary, then, when given an essay question, think about the precise wording and content of the question: is it a relatively open question providing for a range of answers, or has it been designed to yield a more structured response?

Because many Built Environment courses contain an element of professional training, the writing of reports, as distinct from essays, is often included as a form of assessment. After all, in the work environment, the professional is called upon to write up a report rather than an essay! Essays are an appropriate mode for the assessment of subject knowledge acquired through study. As noted above, essay titles are often an invitation to 'discuss' or to 'analyse' an issue or competing viewpoints of a specified topic. Essays allow for a relatively discursive writing style, which encourages the presentation of detailed exposition and argument on the subject topic.

In contrast, the style of report writing is much more concise. Reports are often used as the written assessed outcome of field work or project work that involves practical application as well as theory. While essays are written as a continuous logical argument, with one paragraph smoothly following from the previous one, reports are less continuous in the sense that the content is divided up under separate title headings – and often sub-headings – that communicate the paragraph content visually to the reader. Report writing requires a comparatively terse style that effectively summarises the key points succinctly. Of its nature, a report should be relatively brief and, for this reason, students may be required to submit some of the relevant background workings, findings and data to their main report within attached appendices. In this case, it is important to remember that the primary argument and findings should be in the main report, and that the function of the Appendix is to provide the background materials underlying that primary material.

The general overall structure for both essay writing and report writing is similar, and also similar to some of the points made elsewhere in this chapter with respect to examination technique. The bullet point lists, below, indicate that the structure of a report is more formal than that of an essay. To clarify the distinctions between an essay and a report, the outline structure for each is presented below.

For an essay
- Begin with an introduction that explains the context and refers to related key work – but take care to keep this introductory material relatively brief. This is important so that the introduction does not eat into the time and space available for the main substance of the answer.
- The second step is to state clearly the aim or purpose of the present essay and how it responds to the question.
- The main section should provide treatment of the issue or problem that is the core subject matter, considered critically and from more than one viewpoint.
- Your essay will then be rounded off by a brief concluding section that summarises the main argument and the conclusion(s) that you have drawn from them.
- Summarise the sources upon which you have drawn in preparing your coursework in a closing bibliography at the end of your work. The bibliography contents should be presented clearly in the format used by your study institution.

For a report
- Begin with an introduction that explains the context and refers to related key work – but take care to keep this introductory material relatively brief. This is important so that the introduction does not eat into the time and space available for the main substance of the answer.
- The second step is to state clearly the aim or purpose of the present report and how it responds to the project brief.
- Provide a brief account of the study undertaken, referring to the methodology used, and then present the findings from the study, discussing their analysis and significance.
- Your report will then be rounded off by a brief concluding section that summarises the main argument and the conclusion(s) that you have drawn from them; this conclusion should be accompanied by a clear set of recommendations for action, based upon the data and analysis contained in the main body of the report.
- The main written report should be followed by appendices where appropriate.
- Summarise the sources upon which you have drawn in preparing your coursework in a closing bibliography at the end of your work. The bibli-

ography contents should be presented clearly in the format used by your study institution.

It is helpful, at an early stage in your study when there may only be two or three relevant sources, to begin the habit of formally presenting source material as an attachment to written work. This will help you to get into the routine of expressing source material within the required conventions and make easier the task of listing the bibliography associated with a larger piece of written work such as a long essay or a dissertation.

In addition to the listing of your sources in a formal bibliography it is helpful to reference the more useful sources. Referencing allows you to demonstrate to the assessor *how* you used a particular source in compiling your written work. The reference should appear at the end of the sentence or paragraph or as a footnote, depending on the conventions used by your place of study, and should contain enough summary information about your source to allow the reader to locate the full source reference in the accompanying bibliography. For example, a reference might refer the reader to 'Brown and White, 2003, page 102', while the full bibliography entry provides the details of the full title and the publisher of Brown and White's book on architectural history published in 2003.

8.3.4 Project assessment

Many Built Environment programmes are concerned with the application of principles to practical situations relating to the built environment. The built environment is the real-world 'laboratory', in which ideas can be tested and in which graduates will be working in their future careers. For these reasons, project work often plays a major role in the assessment of learning on Built Environment courses. 'Project' is a generic term that describes activities intended to incorporate real-world problems into the process of student learning. It can cover a wide range of activities, from architectural design work to the appraisal of a company's real estate management strategy. Projects may be on a small scale, especially during the early stages of a programme of study. Alternatively, as students progress through their studies, more ambitious projects can be undertaken, including synoptic projects designed to assess knowledge across more than one component module of the course, in addition to testing a range of student skills. The breadth of the nature of projects means that the means of assessment are equally diverse.

Architectural projects may be assessed through the submission of a portfolio of design work, as discussed in more detail in section 8.3.9 below, about the assessment of visual presentations. In other subjects, projects are often assessed through written reports or presentations, one of the other forms of assessment explained in this chapter, or some combination of these. A combination of means of assessment is often appropriate for larger projects in order to judge the process through which the student has conducted the project in addition to assessing the product or outcome derived from that process. A written report can be a good means of assessing the product, but it is less helpful in illuminating the process undertaken in order to achieve it. For larger projects, assessment of the process may be undertaken during the course of the project in order to provide formative feedback and assist students with successfully undertaking the later stages.

The following core stages in undertaking a project are likely to be reflected in the assessment criteria:

- formulation of the problem/question to be addressed;
- application of theory to the problem/question;
- information and data researched and used;
- overall planning/management/execution of the project;
- presentation, analysis and interpretation of data/results;
- answer to the problem/question;
- conclusions/recommendations/critique of work.

Group-work assessment

The assessment strategy for a programme may well be designed so that most project work is undertaken by individual students, but some selected projects are undertaken by groups of students. Group work provides a good means of assessing teamwork skills and so it is worth remembering that a successful group will consist of a successful team. Sometimes group work will be the precursor to preparing for an individual assessment, and at other times group work will be mirrored in a group mark for the assessment. Where the latter happens, it is important that there is provision for further negotiation of an individual student's mark in the minority of cases where not all members of the group make equivalent contributions to the group work.

Where students are given the opportunity to formulate groups of their own choice to undertake group work, it is important to consider what characteristics make for an effective team. Effective teams consist of people with very different skills and so an effective team may not overlap with a student's immediate circle of friends. As a simple example, where assessment is based upon both the written and the visual presentation of the project findings, a group of three made up of a person with good organisational and project-management skills, another with good writing skills and a third with good visual-communication skills may well be more successful than a group containing two students with very similar skills. So, an effective group will consist of a number of individual students who are able and willing to give equivalent but different contributions to the project and its assessment.

8.3.5 Work-placement assessment

Work-placement experience can be essential to architectural education where a minimum amount of work experience is required in order to progress through the various stages of professional accreditation. It is also important to building and construction management, where it is highly desirable for the student to have obtained actual experience of building and construction processes before graduation. Work placements may be assessed solely on a pass/fail threshold standard, or they may be marked in a manner comparable to other student assessments on the course.

Work placements complement and reinforce academic learning by offering practical experience through which the student can apply and filter the academic content of the course. The application of course content to the work situation enables the student to develop professional practice competencies, in the form of both knowledge and skills. There may be particular aspects that are important to the working environment, such as health and safety when a student works on a construction site. Skills such as the ability to work both independently and harmoniously as a member of a team are likely to be practised and developed during work experience.

The assessment of work placement can therefore extend from assessment of the students' knowledge and skills to assessment of their teamwork capabilities and ability to manage their time so as to achieve their work goals. Assessment can become quite complex where such a broad range of competencies is to be measured. Criteria should be clear and clearly weighted so that the student is aware of the importance attached to different aspects of his or her experience in the context of assessment.

Assessment may take a number of forms. Work-placement activity can be looked at through the use of learning contracts and/or reflective writing, as explained in the following sections. Alternatively it may be assessed through one or more project reports. Or a combination of these methods may be used, depending upon the length and academic objectives of the work placement associated with the course.

The employer may contribute to the assessment of work-based learning undertaken through a work placement. This contribution can take the form of countersigning a student log book to confirm that the student did in fact carry out the logged activities at the times stated. More detailed contributions from the employer can consist of a formal report, upon the students' completion of their work to the employer's satisfaction, commenting upon the relative merits of the students' performance in the work environment.

The student may be required to maintain a log or record of the main activities undertaken during the work placement, in particular those activities that contribute to the attainment of the learning outcomes associated with the placement experience. In addition, a more in-depth report is often required in relation to a specified aspect of the learning achieved from the work placement. Writing such a report should help students to analyse the contribution that the practical experience is making to their professional education.

On work placements, students are often assigned an academic tutor who will oversee the quality of their work experience in order to check that it meets academic expectations, and to check that the student is not running into any significant problems. Where problems do arise, the tutor is available to offer advice to help to resolve the difficulty. In addition, where practical, the tutor will usually make at least one visit on order to discuss progress with both the student and the employer. This visit may also form the basis of part of the workplace assessment.

8.3.6 Learning contracts

Learning contracts act as a valuable means for the assessment of learning in the vocational and professional subjects contained within the Built Environment course. They are especially useful in relation to the work-based, experiential learning introduced in Chapter 6. Such work-based learning may be based upon medium- or long-term student placements or around project work. The aim of the learning contract is to provide a vehicle through which the student can structure and learn from the work experience, with an explicit relationship to the learning objectives of the academic programme of study. Sometimes the outcomes of the learning contract are tailored so that a practical outcome provides a benefit to the working practices of the supporting employer as well as a benefit to the student's learning. For example, a student may provide an updated set of procedures for an activity, or guidelines for producing a database to manage an information set.

In relation to the skills outlined in Chapter 7, learning contracts assess the student's management skills in relation both to project management and also to their personal time management. The reflective process underlying learning contracts also helps to equip students for their continuing professional development. An important element of the learning contract is that the student contributes a major part of the input to the contract and to the nature of the outcomes of be assessed. This is very different from examinations – the students here are partly able to shape their own assessment under the professional guidance of their academic tutor.

The core of a learning contract is a written, negotiated agreement between the student and the academic tutor to the effect that the student will undertake and complete a particular activity during the period of the contract and provide evidence to support the processes through which the activity was undertaken and completed. There is often provision for self-evaluation of the student experience through the requirement for a reflective journal or commentary as an element of the materials to be submitted for assessment.

Where a named workplace mentor is involved in addition to the academic tutor, it is important that the nature of the role and the time and input expected from the mentor is clear. Mentors are people who enjoy undertaking this task but often have limited time in which to undertake it because of the everyday pressures of their work.

There will usually be generic assessment criteria for all the learning contracts to be undertaken by students on a particular module of study in order to ensure adequate consistency of effort and achievement across the differing individual contracts agreed between students and their tutors and also the differing workplace experiences of individual students.

The materials to be submitted for assessment at the end of the learning-contract period will usually have three components. One component is the learning contract itself. As the workplace experience developed, this may have had to be modified from the original proposal and any such modifications should be clear to the assessor. The second component is a reflective journal or commentary offering the student's self-assessment of the learning experience during the learning-contract period. (The reflective journal is explained more fully in section 8.3.6.) The third element is the file containing the relevant materials used in order to achieve the agreed learning outcomes of the contract and, often, a brief formal report relating to the project. The supporting materials will include some academic reference material such as journal articles. However, the nature of experiential learning is distinct from that of learning on campus or online. This means that relevant supporting information from experiential learning may include other elements. These can be completed worksheets demonstrating the student's activities during the work placement, especially those activities that contributed to the achievement of the learning outcomes. Overall plans and project-management charts will also be relevant material to submit for assessment once they are clearly related to the task in hand.

In summary, a learning contract can be successfully completed provided the student concentrates upon the following questions:

- Learning objectives – what have I undertaken to learn through my learning contract?
- Learning strategy – how am I going to ensure that I actually learn this during my work experience?
- Evidence of learning – what evidence do I need to collect during my work experience and how am I going to collect it?

• Assessment criteria – how am I going to demonstrate to my tutor that I have achieved these learning objectives and satisfied the assessment criteria?

8.3.7 Reflective learning and its assessment

The assessment of reflective learning can take a variety of formats. Students may be asked to submit reflective material in the form of a commentary, a journal or a diary. This reflective material may be assessed singly; more frequently it will be considered as one element of a wider assessment. An important role of reflective learning is to equip students studying professionally accredited courses for their own future continuing professional development.

Students may be asked to complete individual reflective work to accompany assessed group work, so that the tutor can evaluate their individual contribution to the group effort. In the case of individual project work, the reflective material may be one component of the project work to be submitted for assessment so that aspects of the student's own learning from the experience of undertaking the project can be assessed. This may form an element of assessment through a learning contract, as described above, or other forms of project assessment.

Whether the format of the reflective material required for assessment is that of a commentary, a journal or a diary, the same general principles apply. Reflection should be undertaken frequently so that the reflective writing indicates the steps forward involved in making the journey from the beginning to the end of the project or piece of work that is subject to the reflection. Reflective writing cannot be effective if it is left until the end, by which time the essential learning points from the early stages will have faded, instead of being fresh memories.

Reflection involves thought about an event or events over a given period in relation to the relevant learning outcomes. In general, the exercise of reflection should consider some or all of the following questions:

• What are the facts/event(s) upon which I should reflect?
• What is their context?
• How do I feel overall about the facts/event(s) upon which I am reflecting?
• What was my role in relation to these facts/event(s)?
• What were my actions in relation to these facts/event(s)?
• What was important about the facts/event(s) overall?
• What was important to me about the facts/event(s)?
• What happened before and afterwards that I need to consider?
• What went well for me and what went less well – indicating where I should concentrate my efforts in order to improve?

Reflective writing can capture some relatively advanced learning skills in that it requires the author to be observant, analytical and self-critical. Effective writing also requires careful thought and prioritisation of the features that are really important and why they are important. Reflection is an effective means of learning – but one that requires some practice in order to generate significant benefits to the student.

8.3.8 Oral presentations

Oral communication skills were discussed in Chapter 7 and these are often assessed through the medium of an oral presentation. Oral presentations may be required in a variety of contexts: for example, as part of the seminar or workshop programme accompanying a module, or in relation to the presentation of a completed project. Students may be asked to give an individual oral presentation, or to present part of a small group exercise. Assessment may be undertaken wholly by the tutor or at least part of the assessment may take the form of peer assessment (see section 8.3.8).

Oral presentations offer an opportunity to assess both the student's competency with regard to knowledge learnt and his or her oral communication skills. In addition, presentations test the student's ability to structure and present an argument effectively. The presentation, like an essay, should have a clear introduction, middle and end, with the main points being adequately explained and illustrated. The presentation exercise may also be designed to allow students to use illustrative material or different media to accompany their verbal presentation. In these cases, the ability to use complementary media and illustrations effectively will also be assessed so that visual, as well as verbal, communication skills are tested through the same exercise. Where the visual material is presented using a computer, then ICT skills can also be assessed through such a presentation format.

Therefore, assessment criteria may relate to the subject content of the presentation, the structure of the material presented, and also the style of presentation including visual materials used.

The visual material will itself be the central feature in instances where architecture students are making oral presentations of their design work. It will play a much smaller role in scenarios where verbal advocacy skills are being encouraged, such as role-play events for example in relation to the law or to construction projects.

8.3.9 Visual presentation

As noted above, assessment through the visual presentation of material is central to the assessment of design work prepared by architecture and urban design students and so is discussed further in the separate paragraphs below. Similarly, building and construction management students will undertake building drawing activities that can be assessed in relation to their visual attributes.

Visual presentations are an appropriate means of testing the visual and graphic communication skills outlined in Chapter 7. In addition to its applicability to the work of architecture and building students, acquisition of these skills and therefore their assessment is relevant to all built-environment professionals. This is because many will need to undertake formal presentations to clients, in which a verbal and written presentation is accompanied by a visual commentary. For this reason, some employers now require candidates to prepare a full presentation upon a prescribed topic as an integral component of their selection process.

Visual presentation can take the form of paper-based artwork and posters or of computer-based presentations. As part of a wider programme-assessment strategy, they play a valuable role in encouraging students to think differently about how to present the results of their work to maximum effect. While thinking about design is a major part of architectural education, it is an important exercise for other students of the built environment. Summarising the outcome of a project through means of a poster can prove an interesting challenge and can also be used as a medium through which to test, and for students to display, IT skills.

For programmes other than architecture, the precise criteria for the assessment of visual display work will vary according to the context of the particular coursework brief. In general, however, it is likely that the following criteria will underlie part of the assessment:

- Is it self-explanatory?
- Is its purpose clear?
- Does it make an effective visual impact?
- Is the level of detail appropriate?

These four points are all aspects of the fundamental point: does the poster or presentation communicate effectively to its audience? Without practice, all four can be more difficult to achieve than you might imagine!

Architectural design projects

Design projects begin on a relatively simple basis, building up to complex design projects for an integrated group of buildings that may require a significant amount of drawing and related work to be submitted for a single synoptic summative assessment. This assessment can represent a substantial proportion both of the student's effort and the student's final course result. It is therefore important that the summative assessment is preceded by an effective formative assessment and learning process so that a large amount of student effort is not misdirected into work that is unlikely to meet the intended learning outcomes of the programme.

In the early stages of development of the design work for a project there may be provision for some individual discussion between student and tutor, or discussion may occur in a wider group setting so that all students can benefit from the tutor's and their peers' comments upon their work in progress.

Once the work is further advanced, it is common for students to have the opportunity to make a combined visual and oral presentation of their work in progress, giving a brief verbal exposition of their work and answering questions from other students and from their tutor. As well as testing the student's verbal presentation skills, this provides an opportunity to check whether the visual presentation is accessible to its audience. Depending upon the project brief, the visual presentation may consist of free-hand drawing, computer-aided design work, a three-dimensional model or a combination of these. Early projects will focus on the design work in its own right, then later in the course, projects provide the opportunity for a synoptic approach, unifying the design with the construction and environment of the building(s). At more advanced levels, tutor and peer review may be supplemented by the involvement of practising professional architects in the presentation and criticism of the student's work in order to assess the developing work against the expectations of the real world of professional practice.

Following these presentations, tutors may take an overview of the standards and merits of the work attained by the students' group overall. This enables general feedback on the strengths and weaknesses revealed in the students' response, to date, to the project brief. Such feedback, combined with individual feedback and an individual indicative mark, provides the necessary direction to allow the students to continue their project work, building upon the constructive criticism received.

The final design work submitted will be assessed by a panel of staff in order to agree the student's summative results for the project. On some architecture courses, this staff panel is supplemented by a small number of elected student representatives, or by a small number of professional architects.

8.3.10 Practical assessment

Practical assessment is the most appropriate means of assessing students' mastery of equipment and its use. It is used in those cases where the tutor needs to be satisfied that the student has attained a minimum threshold standard of competence and may therefore be assessed on a pass/fail basis rather than marked over a range.

One example is where it is necessary to check that all students have acquired the minimum information technology skills required for them to undertake the more advanced components of their course successfully. A further example would be testing of the practical ability of building and surveying students to use surveying equipment, obtain accurate measurements and interpret the results correctly.

8.3.11 Peer and self-assessment

Peer assessment is the process through which students comment upon and mark each other's work. It can be especially useful with regard to formative assessment and is also sometimes used as a minor component of a summative assessment. Where it is used in summative assessment, it is highly desirable that students have the opportunity to be taught and to practise these skills in earlier formative situations.

The objective of peer assessment is to acclimatise students to work situations where judgements about their contributions will be made by a group of peers. Peer assessment helps students to develop their ability to form independent, objective judgements about their own, and others', work. As students have to interrogate the relevant assessment criteria in order to arrive at their judgement, the experience forces them to analyse the criteria and consider "what the tutor is looking for" in greater depth. This process of analysis will contribute to their own learning and ability to undertake informed self-criticism of their own work. Peer assessment is often used as part of the assessment of oral seminar presentations. It also plays an important role in the assessment of design studio work in architecture, where it is used to accustom students to receiving and constructively considering peer criticism and to help students understand and separate the subjective and objective elements of good design.

Peer assessment works best where the foundations for the experience have been carefully laid. Students need to understand how to undertake the process in a professional manner, separating the substance of a peer's work from such influences as friendship or the entertainment value of a student's presentation. They also need to understand both the assessment criteria being evaluated and how to apply these to the work being assessed. Where these conditions are satisfied, peer assessment can contribute to the development of the group and teamwork skills discussed in Chapter 7.

As well as judging each other's work, students are sometimes required to assess their own work. Such self-assessment serves learning objectives similar to those of peer assessment. It encourages students to consider the criteria and standards against which tutors assess their work, and also to make their own judgement as to the extent to which they have individually met these criteria and standards. Experience suggests that self-assessment forms a useful part of encouraging students' reflective learning but that it should be carefully moderated by, and discussed with, the tutor as students are, for the most part, harsher in their self-judgment than are others in judging their performance. Without careful mediation therefore, self-assessment may undermine the confidence of students about their capabilities.

▶ 8.4 Learning, teaching and assessment: summary

Your studies should help you to learn to analyse and to appraise situations and your own experience. As a qualified professional, you should be alert to opportunities both to enhance your own practice but also to enhance that of others.

Hopefully, your studies will have taught you to appreciate the richness and complexity of the built environment. A successful project in the built environment requires the involvement of all the relevant stakeholders, preferably from the project's initiation stage. Your ability to work as part of a team and to coordinate and work across the different contributing professions and interest groups in the built environment will therefore be vital to your successful career.

Employers value the ability to take an overview of a problem, to work inter-professionally, to communicate effectively in a variety of media – written, verbal and visual – to work as part of a team, and also to be committed and enthusiastic. These attributes will stand you in good stead in any career and the built environment is no exception.

For these reasons, Part Three of this book has demonstrated the importance to today's Built Environment graduates of learning from practical problems and projects, and also of acquiring and developing skills as well as knowledge.

Part Four
Study and Practice

9 Academic study and professional practice

> *This chapter investigates the connections between academic study and professional practice within the built environment in the context of a multi-disciplinary and sometimes multinational environment, including the importance of lifelong learning in the information economy.*

Graduates must be aware that academic study often oversimplifies real life, even when curriculum delivery makes extensive use of the project- and problem-based learning discussed in Part Three. Academic study necessarily often focuses upon a single subject discipline: in practice, problems and projects often cross disciplines. Academic projects and scenarios frequently assume that the professional is employed by a friendly and sympathetic client – in reality this is sometimes, but not exclusively, the case!

A successful career in the built environment depends upon a good grasp of academic principles combined with good professional practice experience. University courses rightly concentrate primarily upon providing the academic basis that can act as a solid foundation for the graduate's future career in practice.

▶ 9.1 Practice: the employment perspective

9.1.1 Employment in the built environment

Some graduates will find that their employment primarily allows them to practise within their field of specialisation, as an architect, a planner or a valuer (see Table 9.1). Planners normally have the narrowest range of employment opportunities: for example, around two-thirds of Royal Town Planning Institute (RTPI) members in the UK are employed as planning officers in local government. In this role, many will come into close working contact with real estate managers and also with architects in private practice. Architects' work will frequently bring them into contact with builders – not least when they go on site to inspect the building work that

Table 9.1 Study subjects and areas of employment

Architecture	Landscape architecture
Building surveying	Quantity surveying
Building	Construction management
Planning	Urban design
Real estate management	Facilities management

Table 9.2 Sectors within the built environment

Central government	Local government
Consultancy	Private practice
Developer	
Private sector – construction	Private sector – non-construction
Community/voluntary	Quango

is transforming their design into reality. Many construction managers or urban designers may well find themselves in frequent contact with colleagues in other professions. To a greater or lesser extent, the world of practice is such that the different professions work and interact together: in particular, in areas such as urban design, but also throughout the built environment through joint involvement in projects. This book has aimed to show how these interconnections arise and how studying the built environment can help to prepare graduates for employment in a multi-professional environment.

As a further example of the practical importance of interconnections within the built environment, the sectors that provide employment and provide clients can be shown together. Think of actual examples – look at Table 9.2 and you will find a complex web of possible employer–client linkages across and within these sectors.

Above we have stressed the interconnections but, in practice, recent research (see *www.bettertogether.ac.uk*) has identified the following as continuing barriers to interprofessional working in the built environment:

- professional territoriality;
- organisational structures;
- stereotypical views of other professions;

- issues associated with power and control;
- legislative frameworks;
- lack of resources;
- lack of communication.

One of the main ways of breaking down these barriers is likely to flow from the changing nature of careers and employment in contemporary society. Of the current graduates seeking employment in the built environment, many will change jobs during their working life and some will also change their profession while remaining under the built-environment umbrella. This context of change, rather than continuity, with respect to the particular professional knowledge needed during a working life has implications for the nature of study as a preparation for employment.

Awareness of the role of other professionals in the built environment helps an individual to work smoothly with those other professionals in their employment and to avoid the barriers described above. It also provides useful knowledge of the possibilities available to those employees who find that they do wish to change their professional specialisation during the course of their careers.

Employers also value skills in their employees and many of these are generic across the built environment. For instance, because communication skills are valued by employers in architecture, construction, planning and real estate, students who have acquired and develop these skills will be more readily able to transfer their employment through career change. This serves as a reminder of the importance of studying the skills discussed earlier in Chapter 7.

It has been argued earlier that knowledge in the contemporary world is dynamic and not static. This means that it is not the graduate's store of acquired knowledge that is important to a future employer so much as the ability to update that knowledge and also to find and process new information. The need to have these information skills also affects academic study as a preparation for practice, as discussed further in section 9.3.

▶ 9.2 Practice: the academic perspective

9.2.1 Good practice in higher education

In most countries, the government funds an agency that is intended to enable the generation and dissemination of good practices among the nation's higher education institutions. This is an essential aid to innovation in, and to the enhancement of, the practices that inform the student's educational experience. In some countries, including the UK, generic bodies are also complemented by bodies that cover a single subject, or a related group of subjects. For instance, the UK Centre for Education in the Built Environment (CEBE) works across the subjects covered by this book. Its activities are strengthened as it works in cooperation with a government-funded Academy for higher education.

In addition to the publication of a regular newsletter and regular updating of the information available on the CEBE website, CEBE funds small-scale applied research projects that investigate a wide range of educational issues in the Built Environment, from the shape of the curriculum, to supporting students, to investigating the reasons for the relatively high career drop-out rates of qualified females in the professions.

As well as CEBE, the main professional bodies in the UK and other countries fund conferences to support the exchange of research and ideas. International exchange of ideas is increasingly important as the professions and academia become more global. In Europe, the European Society of Planners Conference attracts participants from a large number of different countries, as does that of the European Real Estate Society.

Interested students can also seek involvement across countries and universities through student exchange programmes. Where these are not offered as a formal component of the programme, there are sometimes funding opportunities available to students interested in spending part of their study time in a different country. In Europe, the SOCRATES programme has supported student exchanges for many years across a wide range of degree programmes, including those in the Built Environment. So, if you are interested, ask for more information and find out what opportunities are available!

9.2.2 Women in the built environment

In most countries the factual position is that women are under-represented within the built-environment professions covered by this book. Equally, they are under-represented on the academic programmes of study that lead into these professions. One objective of the present author in selecting the specialist subject contributors for the book was, quite deliberately, to attain a gender balance in order to raise, even in a small way, the voice of the female academics in the Built Environment.

It has been observed earlier in this book that effective teams are composed of individuals with different skills and attributes. This often means that effective teams are comprised of both genders, as well as of individuals with different personalities. Too often in the built environment, teams are unbalanced because of the absence of females – or the absence of females with an effective voice.

It is recognised that women have a vital contribution to make to effective interprofessional working in the built environment. Employers, among others, increasingly recognise and value women's ability to see the whole picture and to facilitate the operation of interprofessional teams.

At present, however, it is regrettable but true that a high proportion of those females who do complete their qualification as built-environment professionals leave their profession quite early in their careers. This is certainly true of the membership of both the RICS and the RIBA in the UK. The RIBA has recently sponsored research aimed at establishing why this dropout occurs, with a view to ameliorating it. The research concluded that the main reasons why women become discouraged and leave architecture appear to be poor remuneration, long hours of work, the scarcity of female role models, and alleged discrimination by employers when compared with the experience of male colleagues (*Times Higher Education Supplement*, 28 February 2003). The RICS is similarly aware of the need to encourage more women into surveying and has a number of initiatives intended to support raising the ratio of females to males in the profession.

Because, in many countries today, it is as usual for women as for men to undertake study in higher education, the universities offer a secure environment in which women can learn both about the built environment and about their own personal skills and attributes. Concerns about the relatively low proportion of women studying the Built Environment subjects has led universities to review their programmes in order to ensure that the design and delivery of the curriculum are accessible to as many groups as possible: including women, international students and those students with special educational needs such as dyslexia. A course that is well delivered will encourage the development of good interpersonal relationships among the student cohort studying that course and this, in itself, can offer a valuable foundation for the future networking that aids career success in the future.

Overall, however, it is easier to analyse the problem than to advocate solutions – apart from encouraging enough females to persevere so that a critical mass develops who can provide mutual support for female colleagues and provide a future generation of female employers in the built environment.

9.2.3 The initial professional qualification

During the past thirty years, the real estate management profession has changed from one for which the principal route to qualification was part-time study to one for which qualification is obtained through full-time study of an accredited university degree course. This may either be a three-year undergraduate course or alternatively a one-year conversion course for those whose undergraduate degree is in a different – that is, non-cognate – discipline. The formal degree qualification then acts as entry into two years' practical experience with a recognised employer, following which the candidate may present himself or herself for the formal Assessment of Professional Competence. Successful completion of this second stage then allows entry to the profession.

As detailed in section 9.6, most of the built-environment professions require a similar combination of academic study and practical experience before allowing entry into the profession. The length of study required by the professions in the UK varies widely, from the 'three years plus one year' model required by the Royal Town Planning Institute to the three-part seven-year qualification necessary to become a professionally recognised member of the Royal Institute of British Architects.

9.2.4 Continuing professional development

The transition to a largely graduate entry into the built-environment professions has been paralleled by recognition across these professions of the value of continued professional education after initial qualification. This continued professional development (CPD) constitutes an investment in people rather than a cost. It is now widely recognised that CPD yields benefits to both the employee and the employer. This means that the costs of CPD may be shared between the employee and employer, or they may be borne by the employer as an integral part of the company's human resources strategy.

The benefits to the employer derive from a workforce that keeps up to date, in relation to both knowledge and skills, and is therefore more productive. For the employees, this continual updating both helps them to carry out their present job – and also helps to keep them flexible and able to transfer to a different job more readily than would otherwise be the case.

The benefits of further learning, after some practical professional experience has been gained, can be considerable. This is because of the existing experiential learning, in addition to academic learning, upon which students can draw in order to inform their current studies. This is important in deepening study of your specialist profession and can also be important to enhancing your understanding of interprofessional working in the real word of the built environment. Barr (2000, p. 17) summarises the argument in favour of work-based learning as a means of enriching interprofessional education:

> The earlier the interprofessional learning in participants' experience, the less they will have to share and the more the teacher will need to provide. The later the learning, the more the participants should be able to set their own agenda and call upon their own resources. . . . Objectives for inter-

professional education after qualification tend to be more ambitious. Inter-professional education during pre-qualifying studies is typically confined to a module, sequence or placement. Interprofessional education after qualification typically applies to the entire programme.

The professional institutes normally require members to undergo a minimum number of CPD training hours each year as a condition of continued membership. This CPD may be provided by private organisations or through the university sector. Some universities maintain close links with practice and with their alumni, so are well placed to offer CPD either in addition to, or alongside, their offering of more formal postgraduate education.

We have noted earlier that, as students becomes more familiar and confident with their study subject, it is desirable to encourage independent learning and student-directed learning. The extension of this approach is that the student should have a considerable amount of control over their individual CPD experience. This may be facilitated through the use of personal logbooks and/or learning contracts. A good CPD programme helps professionals in the genuine sense of continuing their education and lifelong learning so as to reinvigorate and to enhance their professional practice.

▶ 9.3 Practice in the information economy

9.3.1 Information and research

In today's fast moving world, the built-environment professions must be willing and able to look to research in order to innovate and keep up to date. Research must therefore be seen as, and must become, inclusive rather than exclusive to ensure that it forms an immediate part of professional practice rather than a remote activity confined to the university ivory tower.

Why is this important to contemporary study of the built environment? It is increasingly argued in the Economics and Management literature that successful organisations are those that seek to maximise the value of their intellectual property rather than those that seek to protect it. This is because, in today's dynamic and fast-changing world, current technology and information are ephemeral. The organisation's competitive advantage originates primarily from the value it can derive from that information and technology through the marketplace.

Today, organisations and professions can choose between two strategies. They can protect their information and technology and gain a large share of a small market. Alternatively, they can be more open and gain a smaller share of a larger market. How should they choose? Where positive externalities exist, one advance in an industry triggers positive feedback, leading to further positive externalities. This creates a virtuous circle of expansion in the industry and its market. So a strategy of being open can help to expand the industry and so enhance the individual company's reward because its value expands along with the value added to the industry of which it is a component part. Increasingly the evidence indicates that information and intellectual property are associated with such positive externalities and positive feedback leading to industry growth.

The model outlined here is relevant to many of the producer service industries that act as the current engines of economic growth in the world's richer economies. Where their customers are commercial or public-sector clients rather than private individuals, large parts of the built-environment industry are part of the producer service sector. It is not clear that the full potential for expansion to be derived from being part of this growth sector is yet being achieved by the constituent built-environment professions.

In contrast, where organisations protect and seek to control information, they can retain a large share of industry value – but are less likely to see their industry grow. This latter scenario appears to reflect better much of the built-environment sector today.

If built-environment organisations have been held back by a traditional culture that has led them to seek to control and protect their information, they have (probably unwittingly) held back a wider industry expansion from which they could all benefit. A more open and collaborative approach to research, and to connecting research to practice, would benefit both research and practice.

The traditional approach to research emphasised pure, as distinct from applied, research. A primary objective of research and of researchers was seen as the advancement of pure knowledge. The ensuing products of that research were publications directed at a primarily academic readership not necessarily readily accessible to practitioners. This traditional approach is product oriented, as distinct from process oriented.

Today, an emphasis upon research activity as distinct from research output indicates a broader, more process-oriented approach to research than the traditional approach described above. Research-related skills, as well as research output, and the applicability of these skills to professional practice, suggest a broader approach to research within the context of contemporary higher education learning and teaching. Here the emphasis is upon the normative attributes of academic research as it informs learning, in contrast to the positivist approach outlined above.

A broader approach to research can enhance the contribution of higher education to the non-traditional subject disciplines, including those within the Built Environment. The processes surrounding knowledge and its management are as important today as the knowledge itself. Pedagogy should focus upon the student's learning and upon the ways in which research-active and consultancy-active staff can enable students to acquire knowledge-related skills rather than solely to acquire knowledge.

Many of today's students will embark upon a path of lifelong learning through their continuing professional development. This is recognised in academic study through learning outcomes designed to ensure that graduates are equipped, as independent learners, with the research and information management skills discussed in Chapter 7.

9.3.2 CPD in the learning society

In studying the built environment, continuing professional development, in addition to initial professional education, can therefore play an important role of keeping open the channels of communication for ideas and information to flow in both directions between the universities and practice.

It is important that there is this flow of people and ideas between the universities and practice. A significant part of this flow will comprise graduates and postgraduates from the universities who move into employment within the built environment. In reality the size of the flows of people will be essentially unequal: we can predict a larger flow of people from the universities into employment in the built environment than in the opposite direction.

The following scenario has been earlier depicted by the present author with respect to surveying:

The surveying industry resources and sponsors research and therefore the generation of additional new knowledge in the Universities.

There is a positive impact upon the Universities' teaching of their students.

Students graduate from the Universities with enhanced knowledge that they communicate to their employers in surveying.

The industry benefits from this enhanced knowledge and so is able to fund further research.

This generates a virtuous circle of economic growth for the surveying industry generated by the positive externalities associated with the knowledge economy that are increasingly identified in the economics of innovation but not yet often applied within surveying.

(Temple, 2002)

The built environment as a whole will benefit if it can enable its own expansion by capturing the advantages of a greater two-way flow of ideas and information between the universities and professional practice. This objective could be achieved in a number of ways, ranging from greater research collaboration between the universities and practice, to more active encouragement of knowledge acquisition and knowledge management skills by students, including those students undertaking continuing professional development.

▶ 9.4 The professional institutes and academic standards

9.4.1 Professional-body endorsement

The importance of ensuring that your choice of study programme helps to progress your training for a professional career within the built environment, where this is one of your goals, was discussed in Chapter 2. Here we look in more detail at the different ways in which the relevant professional bodies endorse educational provision, explaining the distinctions in the terminology in current usage.

Where a professional body gives its formal endorsement to a higher education institution to confer a statutory professional qualification, or licence to practise, the relevant academic qualification will have the current and unconditional approval of the professional body.

Many professional bodies accredit academic qualifications where these qualifications confer the holder with credit towards the professional membership to which they aspire.

As noted in Chapter 2, if a professional qualification is important to your career goals, then you must check the current status of your actual or intended programme of study in relation to your preferred professional body. Of course it may be that, for other reasons, a programme of study that does not have the relevant current professional endorsements appeals to you. In this case, you should check directly with the professional body as to whether there is provision for individual membership applications, including the possibility that elements of your study could earn you credit towards your eventual professional membership.

9.4.2 Professional bodies and quality assurance

The professional bodies have their own approach to the quality assurance of those programmes of study in higher education that may be eligible for their approval/accreditation. The extent to which the professional bodies' quality assurance mechanisms are distinct from, or dovetail with, those of the governmental authorities to which the education providers are accountable varies over time and between different countries.

In spite of these variations in practice, the underlying principles are inherently generic. The professional bodies are concerned with quality control: in particular to ensure that the assessment of students ensures a minimum academic standard that is consistent with their benchmark levels of entry to their professional qualification. In this respect, there is little difference between the quality assurance objectives of higher education and those of the professional body, as is explained in more detail in section 5.7.

The professional body may, in addition, seek to ensure the quality of entrants to the profession with respect to their employability in terms of evidence of their professional practice capabilities.

It is normally routine for professional bodies to review their endorsement of programmes of study formally at intervals of about five years. In this way, readers such as potential students can be assured that professional-body endorsement of academic programmes is reasonably current and should not be outdated.

9.4.3 The professional institutes

Those who wish to work within the built environment need to be fully aware of the importance and status of the individual professionals and of the professional institutes of which they are members. Employers respect and demand membership of the professional institutes. Across the built environment, mutual respect for the different professions is, for the most part, high. The only difficulty with this professional respect can be the barrier that it inherently places upon interdisciplinarity and interprofessional working. The individual professional institutes themselves have an important role to play in enhancing an interdisciplinary approach to the built environment.

They also have an important role to play in liaison with the academic providers of built-environment education.

The professional institutes have an important role to play as repositories of knowledge and experience. Experience and wisdom can easily be undervalued and the professional institutes can actively assist in ensuring that experience (and those with that experience) will be valued and disseminated more widely to the benefit of the profession and professional practice. The website addresses for the four main UK-based professional institutes that represent the built-environment professions are listed at the end of the Bibliography section of this book. Meanwhile, the following paragraphs provide a brief introduction to the academic requirements for membership.

Chartered Institute of Builders

There are a variety of routes to membership. Most commonly, in order to gain membership of the Chartered Institute of Builders (CIOB), students need to successfully complete a professionally accredited undergraduate or Masters degree. This is followed by at least three years' relevant experience at managerial level with responsibility for budgets, people and projects. At the completion of this management experience, the candidates must prepare a Report reflecting upon their professional competencies and development, followed by a Professional Interview, to be considered for admission to membership of the CIOB.

Royal Institute of British Architects

The Royal Institute of British Architects (RIBA) has around 30,000 members in the UK and around the world. The education leading to membership of the RIBA is the longest of any in the built-environment professions.

To qualify for professional accreditation, cognate programmes of study must be recognised by both the RIBA and the Architects Registration Board (ARB). A professionally recognised three-year full-time undergraduate degree qualifies the successful student for RIBA Part 1. A further two years of recognised full-time study at advanced undergraduate level is required in order to gain RIBA Part 2. A year's professional experience in an architect's office is normally taken after the completion of RIBA Part 1, followed by a further year of professional experience after RIBA Part 2.

Finally, students are required to successfully complete the RIBA Part 3 Examination in Professional Practice and Management, designed to test professional-practice competencies. Attainment of RIBA Part 3 brings eligibility for registration as an architect with the ARB and for application to the RIBA to become a Chartered Member.

The minimum length of preparation for membership is therefore seven years, and some students take longer to satisfy the requirements for registration.

Royal Institution of Chartered Surveyors

In order to gain membership of the Royal Institution of Chartered Surveyors (RICS), students must successfully complete a professionally approved undergraduate or Masters degree. Graduates must then successfully complete a minimum of two years' structured practical experience before being eligible to take an Assessment of Professional Competence (APC), which must be successfully passed before a candidate may be admitted to professional membership.

In view of the breadth of expertise of its membership, the Royal Institution of Chartered Surveyors also has 16 specialist Faculties, ranging from Construction to Valuation, that its members can join. The RICS has around 110,000 members worldwide and currently operates its links with universities through partnership arrangements.

Royal Town Planning Institute

The Royal Town Planning Institute (RTPI) has members in over 90 countries. The RTPI requires that students complete an accredited undergraduate and/or Masters degree programme, which must encompass elements of both broad spatial planning education and specialist planning education. Masters degrees may deepen the knowledge of graduates who have completed undergraduate Planning degrees. Alternatively, Masters programmes can be designed so as to allow non-cognate graduates to be educated as planners.

Graduates must then successfully complete a minimum of two years' structured work experience before being eligible to take an Assessment of Professional Competence, which must be successfully passed before a candidate may become a Chartered Town Planner. In order to retain members' currency, all members are required to undertake at least 50 hours of CPD in every two-year period.

The RTPI currently operates its links with universities through partnership arrangements.

▶ 9.5 Professional practice in the built environment

Part One of this book opened with consideration of some of the connecting themes that thread through the different Built Environment subjects, and some of the exciting global and local challenges that face the contemporary built environment, such as sustainability and urbanisation. Part Two then looked at the main different subject disciplines that comprise the study of the built environment, followed by Part Three of the book, which focused upon skills and assessment in Built Environment courses.

This final chapter has returned to the theme of the relationship between academic study and the practical world of the built environment. It is therefore opportune in this closing section of the book to revisit briefly the role of those different subjects, with their distinctive professional identities, and of the connections between them in relation to the multi-disciplinary contemporary challenges identified in Chapter 3.

The built-environment professionals necessarily require a depth of knowledge and competence with respect to their specialist discipline. However, this specialist depth should be complemented by a breadth of vision of the core issues facing the built environment. This is necessary so that the context in which the individual professionals apply their specialism to a specific problem is enhanced by their understanding of the wider nature and significance attached to the individual task. Many specific tasks also form a part of wider projects, often the province of a multi-disciplinary, multi-skilled built-environment team. For this reason too, the individual professions need to understand the relationship between their own specialisation and skills and those of the complementary professionals with whom they will work in practice.

It is also important that the student experience of studying the built environment prepares them for a changing world, in which they will need to be multi-skilled and flexible: well prepared to update and adapt their knowledge and skills in harmony with the changes in the built environment and the exciting, if challenging, problems that are faced today and will be faced in the future.

Architects, as the designers of the visual attributes of our built environment, significantly influence the extent to which our urban environment is user-friendly and fits into its social and cultural context. Architects also have a major contribution to make towards sustainability, in relation both to design and also to the materials used in our buildings.

The sustainability or otherwise of building materials and technology will also be highly dependent upon the input of builders and construction managers. In addition, these professionals will have an impact upon the extent to which construction methods are sustainable for the future and appropriate to the local context in which building construction takes place.

Real estate management professionals affect the sustainability of the built environment by the extent to which valuers, developers and property managers take account of the future and of the sustainability agenda through, for example, valuing and actively managing environmental attributes.

Planners will contribute to sustainability in the urban environment by enabling the development of sustainable local economies and urban areas, with effective mixed-use development of housing and employment opportunities. In addition, planners in many countries have an important role to play in negotiating between the public and private sectors.

Building surveyors and quantity surveyors contribute to sustainability through their influence upon the specification of the materials used in the construction process and the combination of these materials through construction techniques.

For urban areas of all shapes and sizes, urban designers will need to keep an overview of the relationships between architecture and planning in the context of urban spatial development. Their ability to take current theories of urban design and translate these into practical spatial realisation will be crucial to sustaining the quality of the built environment.

These summary examples should act as a reminder that all those studying the built environment today with the intention of acting as the built-environment professionals of tomorrow can each have a significant influence upon the quality of the built environment in which we shall all live in the future. Practising the skills and knowledge gained from studying the built environment is one of the ultimate professional challenges in today's world. Responding to that challenge is not easy, but it will be extremely rewarding and should generate a great deal of job satisfaction and a real sense of making a difference to the built environment in which we all live.

Questionnaire for readers

I hope that reading and using this book has helped its readers to think about their personal approach to studying the built environment. This questionnaire is intended to encourage readers to reflect further upon their approach to their future studies.

Personal career plan

What career do you hope to pursue once you have completed your course of study?

Do you have existing work experience relevant to your intended career? If so, is your existing work experience:

- Brief – less than three weeks?
- Reasonable – up to three months?
- Significant – over three months?

Are you interested in adding to your existing portfolio of work experience:

- As part of your course of study?
- When possible in the intervals between periods of study?

Do you need to become a member of one of the professional institutions in order to pursue your career? If so, are you clear as to their membership requirements?

Built environment subjects

What are your main motives for your choice of subjects?

- Personal interest.
- Professional institution requirements.

- I find them easy.
- I enjoy a challenge.
- They build upon my existing knowledge base.

What subject(s) have you already studied?

Which subjects have you enjoyed:

- Most?
- Least?

Which of the subjects that you will study this year do you expect to be most useful in preparing you for your intended career, and why is this?

Which of the subjects that you will study this year do you expect to be least useful in preparing you for your intended career, and why is this?

Are your subject choices constrained by the needs of professional accreditation or is there an opportunity to take one subject or module that would complement your subject profile, such as a different subject in the Built Environment or a language?

Skill development

Look at the following list of ten skills covered in Chapter 7 and categorise them into those that you find easy, manageable and difficult.

- Personal reflection;
- Verbal communication;
- Visualisation;
- Team working;
- Problem solving;
- Information and communication technology;
- Research and information management;
- Written communication;
- Numeracy;
- Management.

Which of the skills that you will learn or develop from your course this year do you expect to be most useful in preparing you for your intended career?

Which of the skills that you will learn or develop from your course this year do you expect to be least useful in preparing you for your intended career?

Assessment

List the following five methods of assessment in your order of preference:

- Essays;
- Professional reports;
- Examinations;
- Group work;
- Visual presentation.

At which modes of assessment do you need to improve most in order to improve your study success?

Bibliography

Those publications listed below are either referred to in the text or have provided background material for the author during the period in which the text was written.

Amin, A., Massey, D. and Thrift, N. (2000), *Cities for the Many, Not for the Few* (Cambridge: Polity Press).

Anderson, J., Shiers, D. and Sinclair, M. (2002), *The Green Guide to Specification*, 3rd edn (Oxford: Blackwell Science).

Anderson, R. I., Loviscek, A. L. and Webb, J. R. (2000), 'Problem-based Learning in Real Estate Education', *Journal of Real Estate Practice and Education*, 3:1, pp. 35–40.

Ashworth, A. (1999), *Cost Studies of Buildings*, 3rd edn (London: Longman).

Avis, M. et al. (1993), *Property Management, Performance Monitoring* (Wallingford: GTI).

Balchin, P. N., Isaac, D. and Chen, J. (2000), *Urban Economics – Global Perspective* (Basingstoke: Palgrave Macmillan).

Barr, H. (1996), 'Ends and Means in Interprofessional Education', *Education for Health*, 9:3, pp. 341–52.

Barr, H. (2000), *Interprofessional Education, 1997–2000: A Review* (London: UK Central Council of Nursing, Midwifery and Health Visiting).

Baum, A. and Crosby, N. (1995), *Property Investment Appraisal*, 2nd edn (London: Routledge).

Baum, A., Mackmin, D. and Nunnington, N. (1997), *The Income Approach to Property Valuation*, 4th edn (London: International Thompson Business Press).

Blowers, A. (1996), 'Town Planning Paradoxes and Prospects', *The Planner*, April, pp. 82–92.

Chapple, M. and Tolley, H. (2000), *Embedding Key Skills within a Traditional University* (University of Nottingham Teaching Enhancement Office; www.dfee.giv.uk/heqe/ks_nottmteo).

Chartered Surveyor Monthly (2001), 'Property in Business', nos. 11 and 12.

Chartered Surveyors Training Trust (2000), *Business Benchmarking* (London).

Commission for Architecture and the Built Environment (CABE) (2001), *The Value of Urban Design* (London: Thomas Telford Publishing).

Construction Industry Board (CIB) (1998), *Degree Courses in Construction and the Built Environment: Common Learning Outcomes*, 10 July.

Construction Industry Task Force (1998), *Rethinking Construction* (London: Department of Environment, Transport and the Regions).

Cottrell, S. (2003), *The Study Skills Handbook*, 2nd edn (Basingstoke: Palgrave Macmillan).

Curzon, L. B. (1999), *Land Law*, 7th edn (London: Pitman Publishing).

Department of the Environment, Transport and the Regions (DETR) (1998a), *Planning for Sustainable Development: Towards Better Practice* (London: HMSO).

Department of the Environment, Transport and the Regions (DETR) (1998b), *Rethinking Construction* (The Egan Report) (London: HMSO).

Department of the Environment, Transport and the Regions (DETR) (2000), *Our Towns and Cities* (London: HMSO).

Department of the Environment, Transport and the Regions, and the Commission for Architecture and the Built Environment (2000), *By Design – Urban Design in the Planning System: Towards Better Practice* (London: Thomas Telford Publishing).

Department of the Environment, Transport and the Regions (DETR) (2001), *Planning: Delivering a Fundamental Change* (London: HMSO).

Department of Transport, Local Government and the Regions (DTLR) (2001), *Reforming Planning Obligations: A Consultation Paper* (London: DTLR).

Greed, C. (2000), *Introducing Town Planning*, 3rd edn (London: Athlone Press).

Greed, C. and Roberts, M. (1998), *Introducing Urban Design* (Harlow: Addison Wesley Longman).

Hamdi, Nabeel (ed.) (1996), *Educating for Real* (London: Intermediate Technology Publications).

Healey, P. (1997), *Collaborative Planning: Shaping Places in Fragmented Societies* (Basingstoke: Palgrave Macmillan).

HEFCE (2001), *Strategies for Learning and Teaching in Higher Education*, Report no. 01/37.

Hoesli, M. and MacGregor, B. (2000), *Property Investment: Principles and Practice of Portfolio Management* (Harlow: Longman).

Hyett, P. (2002), RIBA Presidential Address. www.Architecture.com/go/Architecture/Events 2363.html

Jenkins, A., Blackman, T., Lindsay, R. O. and Paton-Saltzberg, R. (1998), 'Teaching and Research: Student Perspectives and Policy Implications', *Studies in Higher Education*, 23:2, pp. 127–41.

Joseph Rowntree Foundation (2002), *Land for Housing*.

Katz, P. et al. (1993), *The New Urbanism: Toward an Architecture of Community* (New York: McGraw-Hill).

Kostoff, S. (1976), *The Architect: Chapters in the History of the Profession* (New York: Oxford University Press).

Latham, M. (1994), *Constructing the Team*, Final Report of the Government/Industry Review of Procurement and Contractual Arrangements in the UK (London: HMSO).

LeGates, R. T. and Stout, F. (1996), *The City Reader* (London: Routledge).

Lindsay, R., Breen, R. and Jenkins, A. (2002), 'Academic Research and Teaching Quality – the Views of Undergraduate and Postgraduate Students', *Studies in Higher Education*, 27:3.

Lynch, K. (1960), *The Image of the City* (New York: MIT Press).

Macintosh, A. and Sykes, S. (1985), *A Guide to Institutional Property Investment* (Basingstoke: Palgrave Macmillan).

Marshall, D. and Worthing, D. (2000), *The Construction of Houses*, 3rd edn (London: Estates Gazette).

Millington, A. F. (2000), *Property Development* (London: Estates Gazette).

Nicol, D. and Pilling, S. (eds) (2000), *Changing Architectural Education* (London: E. and F. N. Spon).

Oxley, Anne and Glover, C. (2002), *Inter-professional Education*, Occasional Paper 1, FDTL3 'Better Together' (Sheffield: Sheffield Hallam University).

Prince of Wales (1984), RIBA 150th Anniversary Speech: www.princeofwales.gov.uk/speeches/architecture 30051984.html

Prince's Foundation (2000), *Sustainable Urban Extensions: Planned through Design* (London: The Prince's Foundation).

Quality Assurance Agency (1998a), *Teaching Quality Assessment Subject Overview Report: Building* (Gloucester: Quality Assurance Agency).

Quality Assurance Agency (1998b), *Teaching Quality Assessment Subject Overview Report: Land and Property Management* (Gloucester: Quality Assurance Agency).

Quality Assurance Agency for Higher Education (QAA) (2002), *Building and Surveying: Subject Benchmark Statement.*

Ratcliffe, J. and Stubbs, M. (1996), *Urban Planning and Real Estate Development* (London: University College London Press).

Rogers, R. and Power, A. (2000), *Cities for a Small Country* (London: Faber).

Royal Institution of Chartered Surveyors (RICS) (2002), *Property in Business: A Waste of Space?* (London: Royal Institution of Chartered Surveyors).

Royal Institution of Chartered Surveyors (RICS) Foundation (2002), *Red Man, Green Man: Performance Indicators for Urban Sustainability* (London: Royal Institution of Chartered Surveyors).

Royal Town Planning Institute (RTPI) (2001), *The Education of Planners* (London: Royal Town Planning Institute).

Royal Town Planning Institute (RTPI) (2003), *Report of the Education Commission* (London: Royal Town Planning Institute).

Rydin, Y. (1998), *Urban and Environmental Planning in the UK* (Basingstoke: Palgrave Macmillan).

Scarrett, D. (1995), *Property Asset Management*, 2nd edn (London: E. and F. N. Spon).

Scarrett, D. (2000), *Property Valuations* (London: E. and F. N. Spon).

Stansfield Smith, C. (1998), *Strategic Review of Education* (London: RIBA).

Stubbs, M. (2002), 'Car Parking and Residential Development', *Journal of Urban Design*, 7:2, pp. 213–37 (Oxford: Carfax).

Temple, M. (1994), *Regional Economics* (Basingstoke: Palgrave Macmillan).

Temple, M. (2002), 'Education, Research and Practice', chapter 8 in D. Cartlidge (ed.), *New Aspects of Quantity Surveying Practice* (Oxford: Butterworth Heinemann), pp. 259–77.

Thompson, F. M. L. (1968), *Chartered Surveyors: The Growth of a Profession* (London: Routledge and Kegan Paul).

Times Higher Education Supplement (2003), 'Women Failing to Build on Studies', 28 February.

Turok, I. and Edge, N. (1999), *The Jobs Gap in Britain's Cities* (Cambridge: Polity Press).

United Nations (2001), *The State of the World's Cities* (Nairobi: UN Centre for Human Settlement).

United Nations World Commission on Environment and Development (1987), *Our Common Future* (Oxford: Oxford University Press).

Urban Task Force (1999), *Towards an Urban Renaissance*, The Rogers Report (London: E. and F. N. Spon).

Walpole, K. (2000), *The Value of Architecture: Design, Economy and the Architectural Imagination* (London: Royal Institute of British Architects Publications).

Whyte, A. and Edge, M. H. (1999), *Inter-disciplinary Professional Education: Addressing the Uncertainties of Worth and Structure*, ICEE'99, Technical University of Ostrava, Czech Republic: www.fs.vsb.cz/akce/1999/icee99/Proceedings/papers/236

Useful resources

www.bettertogether.ac.uk   HEFCE Fund for the Development of Teaching and Learning (FDTL), project for maximising the benefits of Inter-Professionality in the Built Environment through education and working practices.

www.brookes.ac.uk/LINK   FDTL project into the link between teaching, research and consultancy in planning, land and property management, and building.

www.debs.ac.uk   FDTL project into developing business skills in Land and Property Management Courses.

www.york.ac.uk/org/auril   Association for University Research and Industry Links.

Interested readers can find out more about the activities, membership requirements and academic courses accredited by the main UK-based professional bodies on the following websites:

www.riba.org   and   www.architecture.com   Royal Institute of British Architects

www.ciob.org.uk   Chartered Institute of Builders

www.rics.org.uk   Royal Institution of Chartered Surveyors

www.org.uk   Royal Town Planning Institute

Readers who are seeking further information about education in the built environment or study skills are referred to:

www.cebe.ltsn.ac.uk   Centre for Education in the Built Environment

www.skills4study.com   Palgrave's online study skills resource website

Index